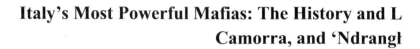
Italy's Most Powerful Mafias: The History and L ░░░░░ ░a
Camorra, and 'Ndrangł

By Charles River Editors

A 20th century sketch of Camorra members

About Charles River Editors

Charles River Editors provides superior editing and original writing services across the digital publishing industry, with the expertise to create digital content for publishers across a vast range of subject matter. In addition to providing original digital content for third party publishers, we also republish civilization's greatest literary works, bringing them to new generations of readers via ebooks.

Sign up here to receive updates about free books as we publish them, and visit Our Kindle Author Page to browse today's free promotions and our most recently published Kindle titles.

Introduction

A picture of the Cuocolo trial, with Camorra suspects in a large cage

"[T]he term mafia found a class of violent criminals ready and waiting for a name to define them, and, given their special character and importance in Sicilian society, they had the right to a different name from that defining vulgar criminals in other countries. - Leopoldo Franchetti, 1876

The word "mafia," Sicilian in origin,[1] is synonymous with Italy, but Italy is home to several different mafias, with three being particularly notorious. While the Cosa Nostra of western Sicily is the most infamous, other powerful groups include the ferocious 'Ndrangheta of Calabria and the Camorra, the third-largest mafia, which is active in Naples and the Campania region.[2] A "mafia" is loosely defined as a criminal organization that is interested in social, economic and political power, combining elements of a traditional secret society with those of a business, but further levels of nuance are necessary in order to understand these groups.[3] In a general sense,

---

[1] According to John Dickie, "mafia" meant something beautiful or "cool" in Palermitano dialect, John Dickie, *Blood Brotherhoods: A History of Italy's Three Mafias* (PublicAffairs, 2014), xxix.

[2] There is also a mafia in Puglia known as the Sacra Corona Unita, and a smaller mafia in Rome, that has been labeled "mafia capitale" (since Rome is the capital of Italy).

[3] Rocco Sciarrone, *Mafie vecchie, mafie nuove: radicamento ed espansione* (Donzelli, 2009).

this is because each mafia creates a myth about the development of the organization, which becomes like an unquestionable truth. In essence, part of what makes its members so completely loyal to it is also what makes outsiders so utterly afraid of it.[4]

It is hard to find an island on the map more central than Sicily. Located at the crossroads between Europe and Africa, and between the Eastern and Western Mediterranean, Sicily has rarely been governed as an independent, unified state, yet the island has always occupied a front-row seat to some of the most important events in history, and nowhere is this more obvious than during antiquity.

Sicily feels like a different country in many ways, and the differences between Sicilians and Italians are much vaster than the tiny geographical separating them might intimate. For example, the linguistic differences between the two are substantial, as Sicilian is practically its own language, rather than just a dialect. It differs from Italian most apparently insofar as the normal final "o" of masculine nouns is replaced by a "u," but beyond that difference, there are lengthy, five syllable words that a standard Italian tongue tends to trip over. In fact, most Italians have difficulty understanding Sicilian if they can comprehend any of it at all.

There is also an ethnic difference between Sicilians and Italians. Most notably, many Sicilians have bright red hair and light eyes, which is usually thought to be a result of the Norman invasions, although today some historians believe it is because of the strong presence of the British during the Napoleonic Wars, as well as the Anglo-American occupation of Italy during World War II. Even Sicilian cuisine varies from the Italian mainland - Sicily is celebrated for having 72 different kinds of bread, and Sicilians often eat ice cream (gelato) for breakfast.

However diverse Sicily might be, it is also paradoxically considered to be an emblem of Italy itself, a paradox it shares with Naples. No writer put it more aptly than the great Romantic poet Goethe. In an April 13, 1787 letter from Palermo, published in Journey to Italy, Goethe made the following declaration: "To have seen Italy without having seen Sicily is not to have seen Italy at all, for Sicily is the clue to everything." As Goethe's words suggest, Sicily is unquestionably unique thanks to its turbulent and rich history, but it shares the same qualities as the Italian nation overall, from its beautiful scenery, delicious cuisine, dazzling sunshine, and unparalleled cultural production to its problems with law and order, and its seeming impenetrability to outside visitors.

Over the course of the 19th century, the people of Sicily found themselves at the center of a struggle for freedom, one that ended up being long and often very bloody.[5] It was during these

---

[4] John Dickie, *Mafia Republic: Italy's Criminal Curse. Cosa Nostra, 'Ndrangheta and Camorra from 1946 to the Present* (Hodder & Stoughton, 2013), xxvi.

[5] James Fentress, *Rebels and mafiosi: Death in a Sicilian Landscape* (Ithaca, NY: Cornell University Press, 2018), 5. To give some context to the unique nature of Sicily's criminality during the early nineteenth century, brigandage was a problem throughout mainland Italy; however, after 1865, it had more or less been brought

crucial years of struggle that the Sicilian mafia, *La cosa nostra* ("Our thing"), started to take shape.[6] The original word "mafia" was a part of Palermitan slang, and although the origins of the word are not completely certain, some linguistic historians believe it originally meant "flashy."[7] One historian of the mafia, Salvatore Lupo, helpfully suggests that it was used in its earliest iterations to vaguely refer to a "pathological relationship among politics, society and criminality."[8]

In response to the rise of the mafia, the Italian state propagated a doctrine of Sicilian backwardness,[9] which they used to introduce martial law and suspend civil liberties, under the pretext that they were not "ready" for the freedoms enjoyed by other Italian regions.[10] Northerners and foreigners mistakenly (and snobbishly) believed that the mafia was just a relic of the primitive, peasant culture that had dominated the island for centuries, and that it was destined to die out once the island had been properly absorbed into the dominant, mainland culture. Others hypothesized that the corruption in Sicilian culture was just a holdover from the Bourbon government and would soon be extinguished once a formal transition was completed.[11]

Of course, they proved to be dead wrong.[12] The Sicilian mafia was not a criminal underworld or a form of political rebellion, but more of a kingdom within a kingdom. In other words, according to historians of the mafia, it was a network of hidden power, an alternative hierarchy that sometimes worked in concert with and sometimes superseded official forms of law and order.[13]

By 1890, the Cosa Nostra had already developed into a sophisticated criminal organization with a great deal of blood on its hands. In fact, its tentacles reached into the highest levels of politics and beyond the borders of Sicily and Italy, traveling across the Atlantic to the United States.[14] Today, their power has been dwarfed by the Neapolitan mafia, La Camorra, yet the Cosa Nostra has continued to wreak havoc in Sicily. In 1992 they were responsible for one of the most high-profile assassinations in Italy since the fall of fascism.

Ironically, the murderous actions of a small segment of society have caused the Sicilian people in general to be perceived as "mafiosi,"[15] even though the vast majority of them have been victims rather than perpetrators.

---

under control – except on the island. Riall, 4.

[6] Dickie, 38.

[7] Fentress, 6.

[8] Salvatore Lupo, *History of the mafia* (New York: Columbia University Press, 2011), 31.

[9] On the history of "backwardness" as a paradigm for northern rule of Sicily, see Riall, esp. introduction.

[10] Fentress, 7.

[11] Riall, 2.

[12] Lupo, *History of the mafia*.

[13] Fentress, 7.

[14] Dickie, 15.

[15] Dickie, 16.

The history of Naples is long and tortured, or at least for centuries that was how its history has been told.[16] Inhabited almost continuously from the Neolithic era to the present, Naples was founded by the Greeks and conquered by the Romans. After the fall of the Roman Empire, Naples passed between various foreign rulers for its entire history prior to Italian unification. Starting in 1040, when the Norman French invaders conquered Campania, Naples was ruled in a dizzying succession by Germans, then French, then Spanish, then Austrians, then Spanish, then French, and then Spanish.[17]

Although it is in many ways a microcosm of European history with a revolving door of conquerors, historians like to stress the unique status of Naples thanks to these diverse influences and unique geography. Set on a bay that provided a natural harbor, Naples is home to Mount Vesuvius, the only active volcano on the European mainland.[18] When Vesuvius erupts, the Neapolitans pay the price, and it has earned its reputation as the most dangerous volcano in the world. However, the threat posed by Vesuvius is tempered by a great benefit: Naples is blessed with extremely fertile soil.[19]

The natural harbor of Naples and its position on the southwest coast of Italy helps explain its history of multiple rulers, insofar as it made Naples a central locus of trade between Italy, Greece, Byzantium, North Africa, Spain, Holland, Flanders, and Germany. Due to its strategic importance, Naples reached high levels of prosperity, and for the same reason, it also suffered as various foreign powers vied for control of the city and the surrounding area.[20]

All the while, the sheer beauty of the bay of Naples, with Vesuvius looming in the distance, has made Naples a place of endless fascination. It boasts imposing castles and fortresses, as well as twisty, turning medieval streets that are home to some of Italy's poorest and most maligned residents. Across the bay are the islands of Capri and Ischia, which only add to the allure of the city. Furthermore, its cuisine – particularly its pizza (which was invented in Naples)[21] and its richly sweet desserts – rates amongst the most appreciated in all of Italy, no doubt thanks to the fertility of the soil that favors agricultural production.

Nonetheless, Naples does not enjoy an excellent reputation, within the context of Italy or of Europe. High rates of petty crime, a decaying urban fabric and the infamous presence of the mafia (known in Naples as the Camorra)[22] all combine to ensure fewer tourists venture to

---

[16] Pietro Colletta, *History of the Kingdom of Naples: 1734-1825* (London: T. Constable and Co., 1858).

[17] Alwyn Scarth, *Vesuvius: A Biography* (Princeton: Princeton University Press, 2009), 3.

[18] Darley, 7.

[19] Scarth, 1.

[20] Cordelia Warr and Janis Elliott, "Introduction: Reassessing Naples (1266-1713)," in *Art and Architecture in Naples, 1266 - 1713: New Approaches*, ed. Cordelia Warr and Janis Elliott (Hoboken, NJ: John Wiley & Sons, 2010), 1–15.

[21] Antonio Mattozzi, *Inventing the Pizzeria: A History of Pizza Making in Naples* (New York: Bloomsbury Publishing, 2015).

[22] For the sensational, definitive account of the global workings of the Camorra, see Roberto Saviano, *Gomorrah: A*

explore Naples, and many Italians (civilians and politicians alike) consider it the ultimate "problem city."[23] Nonetheless, it bears keeping in mind the words of one of Naples' foremost historians, John Marino, who noted, "Naples, like each of Italy's cities, [is] unique, but far less different than is generally believed."[24]

In the particular case of the Camorra, the difficulty of understanding an underground criminal association is made all the more intense because it is so heterogeneous in terms of its development, its different functions, and the diversity of economic sectors in which it operates. To reflect that diversity, some scholars like to refer to it as *Camorre*, the plural version of Camorra. This decision is more than just a question of semantics, because using the plural form helps emphasize the internal differences and conflicts within the Neapolitan mafia, which, in turn, helps explain the very nature of the organization itself. The Neapolitan mafia is famous for its pervasive nature, which is due to the fact that it is organized in a horizontal, decentralized way. This means there is not one single "boss" who dictates policy and can be more strategic in how and when violence is deployed. Unlike other mafias, in the Camorra there has been no long-term reigning family, nor extensive coordination between families to form an alliance and function as a unified mafia for their shared benefit.[25]

Despite all the difficulties in studying (and of course, of prosecuting) the mafia, scholars have made important inroads into understanding how the mafia functions. [26] The main theme that emerges is that the Camorra is engaged in multi-layered violence. The most obvious kind of violence perpetrated by the Camorra is physical violence, which apparently has a concrete series of professional objectives, including to offend and scare enemies, enforce or violate deals, attack or protect businesses, preserve reputations, claim control over a certain area, and to influence the behavior and loyalties of others, from rivals to politicians to ordinary citizens. At the same time, however, the violence of the Camorra has a symbolic meaning, as they choose forms of violence that communicate certain messages. Whether they choose to perform spectacular murders or covert ones, the Camorra is always speaking through its violent actions, and even the choice of weapon - from pistols and sawn-off shotguns to Kalashnikovs, bazookas and explosives - is

---

[23] *Personal Journey into the Violent International Empire of Naples' Organized Crime System* (New York: Farrar, Straus and Giroux, 2007). For the history of the Camorra in a broader context, see Tom Behan, *The Camorra: Political Criminality in Italy* (New York: Routledge, 2005).

[23] Ruth Glynn, "Naples and the Nation in Cultural Representations of the Allied Occupation," *California Italian Studies* 7, no. 2 (2017).

[24] John A. Marino, *Becoming Neapolitan: Citizen Culture in Baroque Naples* (Baltimore, MD: Johns Hopkins University Press, 2011), 114.

[25] Monica Massari and Vittorio Martone, "Doing Research on Mafia Violence: An Introduction," in *Mafia Violence: Political, Symbolic, and Economic Forms of Violence in Camorra Clans*, ed. Massari Massari Monica and Vittorio Martone (New York: Routledge, 2018), 4.

[26] On the methodology for conducting such studies from a political science perspective, see Giacomo Di Gennaro and Antonio La Spina, "Introduction. The Costs of Illegality: A Research Programme," in *Mafia-Type Organisations and Extortion in Italy: The Camorra in Campania*, ed. Giacomo Di Gennaro and Antonio La Spina (New York: Routledge, 2018).

made for a specific reason.[27]

Since the Neapolitan Camorra is not a single organization, and because it developed in the dynamic environment of urban Naples, it has been the most fluid of all the Italian mafias in its development over time. Since World War I, it has been considered a world of gangs that associate and dissociate as needed, joining and splitting as they found it necessary, according to whatever objective they had at the time. For this reason, the senior members of the Camorra on average have shockingly short lifespans, especially compared to their Sicilian counterparts. They also lack the official titles, ranks and rituals of the other mafias. However, they do not appear to need them to be able to control large patches of territory in the Campanian countryside, as they manage to dominate bootleg industries, such as DVD and counterfeit designer fashion production, as well as waste management industries that have turned the beautiful southern Italian landscape into a toxic wasteland that is poisoning its inhabitants.[28] They are also involved in activities that are particularly hard to prosecute, for example, online gambling sector—a sector that involves people from all over the globe using a variety of means to manipulate and defraud users, who are also located all over the globe.[29]

Despite the lack of formal titles, the Camorra clans do have a loose form of organization. Known today as "the System," various nodes are centered around a single, charismatic boss who selects and supervises a range of men who have different jobs, such as zone chief, assassin, and/or drug wholesaler. He pays these men wages, and he generally sets aside a part of the profits in order to help pay families a sort of insurance policy, to help ensure continued loyalty should one of their men be sent to prison. At the center of the system are bonds of kinship, the glue that holds together the Camorra's clans.

Rather than being presided over by a senior man, as is the case in the Cosa Nostra, however, a clan is made up of a cluster of male relatives of about the same age, along with neighbors, friends and their relatives.[30] Each Camorra clan operates much in the same way as a family business, albeit an "extended family." They forge alliances based on kinship as well as economic activities, which allows them to create a durable fabric of diversified sectors and membership. To understand the Camorra is to understand the very specific social and economic context in which it operates at any given moment.[31]

Unlike their Sicilian counterparts who tended towards formal, somber (even old fashioned) dress, one of the Camorra bosses' signature trademarks is their fondness for showing off by

---

[27] Massari and Martone, "Doing Research on Mafia Violence: An Introduction," 2.

[28] Dickie, *Blood Brotherhood,* xli.

[29] Luciano Brancaccio, "Violent Contexts and Camorra Clans," in *Mafia Violence: Political, Symbolic, and Economic Forms of Violence in Camorra Clans*, ed. Monica Massari and Vittorio Martone (New York: Routledge, 2018), 143.

[30] Dickie, *Blood Brotherhood,* xli.

[31] Brancaccio, "Violent Contexts and Camorra Clans," 136.

wearing gangster bling. They have had gold accessories and expensive shirts since the 19th century (and even managed to get themselves such fashion accessories within the prisons where they first operated), and today they also have fancy cars and motorcycles. The sign of a boss was that he drove a Honda Dominator.[32]

This desire to show off is also apparent in the way the Camorra handled its identity, in contrast to the other two main Italian mafias, in the early period. While the Sicilian mafia had many names until "Cosa Nostra" finally took hold, and the Calabrian 'Ndrangheta preferred to avoid being labeled at all (the name 'Ndrangheta first stuck in the mid-1950s), the Neapolitan mafia was always known as the Camorra, and it made no effort to keep its work secret. Every citizen of Naples seemed to know all about it from the very beginning.[33]

While all three mafias have initiation rituals dating to the 19th century, the oldest of the three belongs to the Camorra. The rituals date back to 1850, as the Camorra was taking shape in the prisons of southern Italy. In this simple but profound ritual, the new member was told to take an oath over crossed knives and then made to have a dagger fight with another man (either another possible initiate or a current member). However, the blades would be wrapped leaving just the point exposed, so that the only objective would be to draw a faint trace of blood, after which the fight would end. This ritual ceased in 1912, around the time that the Neapolitan Honored Society dissolved itself,[34] and as it reconstituted itself in various formations over the course of the century, it never again returned to those more antiquated rituals. Instead, the group began to exist more as a loose network of criminals, all working for their own enrichment.

The 'Ndrangheta (pronounced an-*drang*-et-ah) is a close neighbor of the Cosa Nostra and currently considered the most powerful (and difficult to spell) criminal organization in Italy. The 'Ndrangheta is centered around Calabria, the most southwestern region of Italy, almost touching the Sicilian city of Messina. Though it began as far back as the late 19th century, it was not until the 1950s that the 'Ndrangheta started to spread its tentacles throughout Italy and then across the entire globe, forming an empire that now ranges from Australia and Turkey to Chile to Canada.

The fact that the 'Ndrangheta is overshadowed by the Sicilian Cosa Nostra, as well as by the Neapolitan mafia, the Camorra, allowed it to grow and develop outside of the public eye. For years, people actually considered the Calabrian mafia to be part of the Cosa Nostra as a mere appendage, rather than its own entity. This false belief was perpetuated by the high-profile Sicilian pentito, Tommaso Buscetta,[35] and it was not until the beginning of the 21st century that the 'Ndrangheta came into the public eye due to two dramatic killings, the assassination of a politician and the "Duisburg massacre" in a small German village. Nonetheless, the 'Ndrangheta

---

[32] Dickie, *Blood Brotherhood,* xli.

[33] Dickie, *Blood Brotherhood,* xxx.

[34] Dickie, *Blood Brotherhood,* xl.

[35] See Federico Varese, *Mafias on the Move, How Organized Crime Conquers New Territories*, Course Book (Princeton: Princeton University Press, 2011), 31, https://doi.org/10.1515/9781400836727.

is actually the second oldest mafia in Italy, and, despite its origins in Calabria, the poorest region of Italy, it is the wealthiest of Italy's illegal criminal organizations.

Given that people have always been less familiar with this organization, studies on the 'Ndrangheta have also lagged behind work done on the Camorra and the Cosa Nostra. The government took an early interest in the Camorra and Cosa Nostra, creating a paper trail that does not exist for the 'Ndrangheta, and the region of Calabria suffered numerous earthquakes that destroyed what little archival evidence there was available. Of course, the 'Ndrangheta places a premium on secrecy, and thus far it has only had an extremely low number of traitors who were able to testify to the organization's inner workings. Finally, the fact that the 'Ndrangheta is essentially a plural organization makes it very hard to delineate the parameters of what constitutes an 'Ndrangheta cell and what is simply gang activity.[36]

Italy's Most Powerful Mafias: The History and Legacy of the Cosa Nostra, La Camorra, and 'Ndrangheta examines how some of the world's most famous mobs formed, their inner workings, and the events that made them feared around the world. Along with pictures of important people, places, and events, you will learn about the three mafias like never before.

---

[36] Letizia Paoli, *Mafia Brotherhoods: Organized Crime, Italian Style* (Oxford University Press, 2008), 30.

Italy's Most Powerful Mafias: The History and Legacy of the Cosa Nostra, La Camorra, and 'Ndrangheta

About Charles River Editors

Introduction

The Sour Origins of the Cosa Nostra

The 19th century writer E.A. Freeman described Sicily as "the central island of the civilized world" (Freeman 1891: 49). While this description is dated, it emphasized the importance of Sicily's position, located at the center of the Mediterranean Sea between Italy and Africa. It controls the pass between the Eastern and Western Mediterranean by sea, the pass between Italy and Europe to the north, and Tunis and Africa to the south by land. Sicily is furthermore the largest island in the Mediterranean. Its shape is practically like a triangle, with angles pointing west, northeast and southeast, and the tip of its western point slightly cut off. To the northeast, Sicily is located so close to Italy (the crossing between the tip of Italy's "boot" and the northeastern point of Sicily at its narrowest is less than two miles wide) that it was believed in ancient times to have once formed a contiguous landmass with the mainland (Freeman: 51-54; Polybius, *Histories*, I, 42).

A map highlighting the location of Sicily

In antiquity, the island of Sicily was very fertile and suited for agriculture. It was rich in wine, and, especially, in grain. Thus, it should come as little surprise that the worship of Demeter, the goddess of agriculture, was widespread on the island. Sicily was also famously rich, both in mythological and in historic times, in livestock, with many sheep and cattle (tangentially, it was one of the birthplaces of bucolic poetry in the 4th century BCE) and fast horses. Several Olympic victories for Sicilians are recorded, especially in chariot-racing and horse-racing events (Freeman: 91-96).

Despite its fertility, however, the island as a whole is also very mountainous. There was always a strong a division between the coasts and the interior of the island: in the Classical period, colonists like the Greeks and Phoenicians tended to keep to the coasts, while the interior of the island was inhabited by more or less independent native states for a very long time (Freeman: 54-56). In later times, armies wishing to avoid capture or confrontation would pass through the interior of the island, and revolts would almost invariably make their headquarters in one of the inland cities.

To refer to Sicily is actually to refer to a fair number of other small islands that surround it at various distances, all of which were formed thousands of years ago by the volcanic activity beneath the surface of the sea. To give a brief orientation, off the western coast is the Aegadian group of islands, that includes Favignana of the famous mattanza (tuna hunting) tradition. These islands were the site of the Romans' decisive victory over Carthage in the First Punic War. Off the northern coast are the seven Aeolian Islands, including Lipari, the largest island and currently a major tourism hub. They are volcanic in origin and form a subterranean link between the major volcanoes of Etna (on Sicily) and Vesuvius (near Naples). One of the seven Aeolian Islands, Stromboli is still regularly active; it spews streams of lava on its small population to the delight of the tourists who regularly trek up its fertile slopes. In addition to being famous for their intense winds that actually can cut off the two most distant islands from the outside world, these islands produce Sicily's famous green salty caper berries and are also rich in pumice stone. To the north west of Sicily is the island of Ustica, an ancient settlement and rocky island that served as a penal colony until the 1950s. The island of Pantelleria, also a former penal settlement, is found south west of Sicily; its volcanic origins have made it a famous destination for hot mineral springs. Inhabited since early antiquity, Pantelleria was home to Neolithic settlers who constructed ramparts and tombs with the blocks of lava readily at their disposal. Most prominent in recent news is the island of Lampedusa which is found south west of Sicily, and which was likely given its name (rocky in Greek) because of its rugged terrain. The southernmost part of Italy, it is closer to Tunisia at 70 miles away than to Sicily at 127 miles away. Due to its proximity to Africa, it is a frequent landing point for refugees fleeing Libya.

Ben Aveling's picture of Mount Etna

Today, Sicily has a population of around five million people in total, compared to the 60 million inhabitants of Italy; remarkably, its population has only grown about five times the size it was during the Roman Empire. This relatively small population growth is attributable to the fact that a large part of the inner island is inhospitable. This topographical limitation was never overcome, no doubt thanks to the years of harsh rule from various foreign invaders who thought more of their own interests than the consistent development of the Sicilian economy. Thus, Sicilians emigrated in large numbers, contributing to a vast global diaspora that left the population of Sicilians living on the island relatively small in comparison.

Sicily started the 19th century as a Spanish holding and ended it as a part of the Italian nation, but the fact that Sicily went through three different regimes over the course of the 19th century has risked obscuring a fundamental source of continuity throughout. In fact, historians tend to forget that the Bourbon monarchy, the dictatorship of Giuseppe Garibaldi, and the unified Italian government all displayed similar attitudes towards Sicily, adopted similar policies towards the island, and enacted them poorly. They all attempted to try to control the island not by making a formalized, centralized apparatus, but by making informal bargains with the local aristocratic class. The fact that three different kinds of rulers all tried and failed to govern Sicily suggests there was something wrong with the governing strategies, not the Sicilians themselves, but nonetheless, the island earned itself the unfair reputation of being veritably ungovernable. Amongst the Italian liberal government, it was considered a place where ambition went to die, and where all efforts of reform were due to failure because of the violent, impenetrable nature of the society. Neither bureaucrats nor soldiers could bring Sicily into the fold.[37] Northerners blamed these failures on the nature of the Sicilian people themselves; as organized crime began to flourish, they thought that the newly formed shadow state was a vestige of its medieval past that had yet to die. However, the northerners themselves were in large part to blame, for they lacked an understanding of the people they were seeking to incorporate, and they were also attempting to incorporate the Sicilians as subordinates.

In the years before unification, Sicilian society was in constant turmoil. In 1812, nervous nobles decided to draw up a constitution which declared Sicily an independent state to be ruled by its own monarch.[38] They even created a Parliamentary system with representation for the different regions as well as the church. However, they proved ineffectual at governing, and in 1816, the kingdoms of Naples and of Sicily were officially merged to form the Kingdom of the Two Sicilies, governed by none other than the despised King Ferdinand IV of Naples.

In 1848, the island attempted to declare its independence, coming during a year that marked widespread revolt and revolution throughout the entire European continent. In this, Palermo was at the forefront as students at the university began rioting, and the whole island was quickly caught up in the spirit of protest. The successful uprising of 1848 then served to ignite in the hearts of Sicilians the desire for unification that would come in just twelve short years.[39]

When Giuseppe Garibaldi landed in Marsala, Sicily in 1860 with his 1,000 volunteers (known as Redshirts), he declared an end to Bourbon rule and declared that Sicily would be a part of the new Italian nation under his rule.[40] Palermo formally became an Italian city on June 7, 1860, and the withdrawal of the Bourbon forces from the harbor constituted one of the greatest military achievements of the century, astonishing the rest of Europe.[41] Just four months later, Garibaldi went from his conquest of Palermo to the whole of Southern Italy, after which he began preparing to take Rome from the pope and make it the capital of a united Italian nation.

---

[37] Riall, 1.

[38] Gregory, *Sicily. Sicily and England. A Sketch of Events in Sicily in 1812 & 1848. Illustrated by Vouchers and State Papers.*

[39] Sammartino, 104.

[40] Denis Mack Smith, *Modern Italy: A Political History* (Ann Arbor, MI: University of Michigan Press, 1997), 23.

[41] John Dickie, *Cosa Nostra: A History of the Sicilian Mafia* (New York: St. Martin's Press, 2015), 35.

Garibaldi

In many ways, it is fair to argue that the seeds of Italian unification (known in Italy as the *Risorgimento* or "resurgence") were planted in Sicily, yet its role as a point of origin did nothing to make the process of unification any smoother for the fiercely independent island.[42] Mainland Italians, particularly from the north, did not know what to make of their new countrymen. They discovered in Sicily a land with low standards of living dependent on an agricultural economy. That was certainly true, but Sicily's new rulers also were blinded by stereotypes and prejudices.[43] Prime Minister Camillo Benso Cavour even told Parliament that he believed Sicilians spoke Arabic.[44]

---

[42] Riall, 1. On Sicily in the Risorgimento, see also Rosario Romeo, *Il Risorgimento in Sicilia* (Rome: Laterza Editore, 1973).

[43] On the various myths and stereotypes about Sicily, see Giuseppe Giarrizzo, *Mezzogiorno senza meridionalismo: la Sicilia, lo sviluppo, il potere* (Venice: Marsilio Editore, 1992).

[44] Caroline Moorehead, *Human Cargo: A Journey Among Refugees* (New York: Henry Holt and Company, 2007), 76.

This kind of ignorant attitude on the part of the ruling class was sometimes openly hostile and sometimes veiled with romantic attachment, but through it all, it was to characterize the entire process of incorporation of Sicily into the Italian state and would directly contribute to the rise of the Sicilian mafia.[45] Many Sicilians resented the interventions of northerners, who were said to have brought to the island just two things: taxation and mandatory military service. Following unification, emigration rates skyrocketed in Sicily as many Sicilians sought to flee poverty and conscription. The question of taxation was particularly vexing, insofar as the people tended to believe that the fact that they had overthrown the Bourbons through a patriotic rebellion should have somehow exempted them from paying taxes.[46]

Another unanticipated problem was caused by the change in the economic system that occurred when the Bourbon government was dismantled. The Bourbons had actually favored the poor in their economic policies, for instance by depressing the cost of bread via a prohibition on exporting grain. As a result, when a free market was created after 1861, agricultural prices naturally rose. This was considered economic progress as Sicily was inducted into a free trade market rather than depending on a paternalistic system; but the dramatic change in policy affected the poorest members of society in a devastating fashion, which served to create widespread resentment towards the newly formed Italian state.[47]

By 1866, the Italian government was facing another revolt in Palermo, one eerily resembling the rebellion that had defeated the Bourbons. Revolutionary gangs descended upon the city, using the surrounding hills as their camps. Public fear was at a high, as rumors of cannibalism and blood drinking (albeit uncorroborated) flew through the city. The Italian government responded by imposing martial law, but it took an entire decade before Sicily managed to incorporate itself functionally into the Italian state. Finally, in 1876, its politicians were able to enter into a new coalition government in Rome.[48]

Although the Cosa Nostra is now the most notorious of the Italian mobs, there were and are other highly organized, widespread criminal gangs labeled as "the mafia" within Italy itself, including the Sacra Corona Unita in southeastern Puglia, the 'Ndrangheta in southwestern Calabria, and the Camorra, located in and around central, southwestern Campana, specifically Naples and the surrounding area. Thus, even though it is not the oldest of these illegal organizations (the Camorra predates it by a few years), the Sicilian mafia remains the most famous in large part because it gave rise to the most illustrious American mafioso, including Lucky Luciano and Al Capone. It is for this reason that the organization's name is given to these networks worldwide.49 Originally Palermitan slang, "mafia" may have once meant "flashy."50

---

[45] Gino Bedani and B. A. Haddock, *The Politics of Italian National Identity: A Multidisciplinary Perspective* (Cardiff, UK: University of Wales Press, 2000), 93.
[46] Dickie, 36.
[47] Mack Smith, 35.
[48] Dickie, 37.
[49] Dickie 2015:21

A more complex definition explains that the word functions as a catchall phrase, evoking a "pathological relationship among politics, society and criminality."[51]

As it developed into a complex criminal network, the Cosa Nostra also became an organization that perfected the art of getting away with murder. It has functioned simultaneously as a shadow state with ambitions of territorial control, an illegal business aiming to make a profit, and a secret society initiating its members into a code of silence, making its history notoriously difficult to glean.

Northern Italians getting to know the region were troubled by news of a growing criminal network, known as the mafia, but dismissed it as further evidence of Sicilian backwardness, a remnant from the primitive, peasant culture that had dominated the island for centuries. Thus, they searched for its origins within the interior of the island, where the most ancient, agrarian hold-overs remained. They believed that these areas would give up their criminal ways once they were modernized.[52] One optimistic government official predicted that the mafia would disappear once the whistle of a train was heard on the island.[53] Others blamed the criminality on the clash between the ruling barons and the Neapolitan Bourbon government, positing that it would be extinguished once the formal transition to Italian state was completed.[54]

Though the snobbish Italian government had placed the mafia's origins in the past and in the interior of the island, they wasted valuable time looking at the wrong time and place, because the Cosa Nostra was coming into existence and consolidating power at that very moment in a citrus grove in the area of Palermo. In its most powerful years, the mafia was associated with industries such as construction or narcotics trafficking, an image owing much to the flashy Hollywood portrayals, but the Cosa Nostra formed its true entity due to its relationship to the lucrative citrus fruit industry, precisely during the time of social unrest after Italian unification.

Citrus fruits have grown on the island since the 9th century thanks to innovation by Arab settlers, but it did not become a valuable export until the late 18th century, when the British Royal Navy began to buy Sicilian lemons as a cure for scurvy and British tea producers took an interest in using bergamot oil (bergamot is another citrus fruit) to flavor their Earl Gray tea. Sicilian citruses were popular exports before citrus was well-known on the island itself, and exports to London and New York grew at a rapid clip, from 400,000 cases in 1834 to 750,000 by 1850 and 2.5 million cases by the mid-1880s. Thanks to this incredible market, Sicilian citrus groves soon became the most profitable agricultural land in Europe.

This profitability was not the only reason the citrus industry became a natural target for

---

[50] Fentress 2018:6
[51] Lupo 2011:31
[52] Lupo 2011
[53] Dickie 2015:38
[54] Riall 1998:2

criminality - there was another key detail making them the perfect starting point for the Cosa Nostra. Lemon trees were extremely expensive to plant and took eight years before bearing fruit and showing a return on the initial outlay, ensuring that only a small elite could venture into the citrus business. Moreover, lemon trees are a naturally vulnerable species, desperately requiring the Arab's advanced irrigation technology; a relatively minor act of vandalism could undo years of patient waiting. These two elements, along with the high-profit margin and risk levels gave the Cosa Nostra the perfect opening to develop its infamous protection rackets.

The fact that the lemon groves were located around Palermo, the most populated area at the center of the island, was another reason for the mafia to spring up there - concentrated in that area was a vast amount of money circulating and real estate transactions.[55] Furthermore, it boasted a major port, allowing it to be a hub of activity, both legal and illegal. This is another way in which the northern Italian government missed the mark: while they were looking for the criminal activity's ancient, rural origins, a contemporary, highly-connected organization was blooming, thanks to the most modern elements of society.[56]

Historians are able to recount the start of the mafia in the citrus groves of western Sicily thanks to the testimony of a respected surgeon, named Dr. Gaspare Galati, who reported on key details behind how the mafia developed its protection racket. Dr. Galati's involvement with the mafia began in 1872 when he was required to manage his daughters' inheritance. Their main acquisition was a lemon and tangerine fruit farm fifteen-minutes outside of Palermo, known as Fondo Riella. Their newfound property was a technological marvel, with a steam pump used to water the trees. Despite this apparent prosperity, there was something fishy about the way Dr. Galati's brother-in-law, the former owner, had died. Dr. Galati knew his relative had received threatening letters, thanks to information he acquired from the steam pump operator. The author of the letter was the warden of the grove, whose unethical practices belied his desire to run it out of business to take it over as his own. For example, common practices dictated that lemons were paid for even before they matured to mitigate the high cost of running the grove, but Dr. Galati noticed that lemons had started vanishing from the trees, giving his business a terrible reputation.[57]

Fed up with the unethical behavior, Dr. Galati fired his warden and received mysterious warnings from his friends to take the man back. He refused, and the warden's replacement was soon found, shot dead in the grove. When Dr. Galati took his suspicions to the police, he was shocked that they ignored his lead and arrested two random men instead, starting a pattern of police complicity in mafia affairs that would become a lynchpin of the organization. Dr. Galati hired a new warden and received more written threats, but when he took them to the police, he experienced the same lackluster response. Taking the matter into his own hands, Dr. Galati

---

[55] One of the earliest researchers of the mafia, Pasquale Villari, observed that the true Mafia is found where "the greatest estates are to be found" (Dainotto, 2015, p. 25).
[56] Dickie 2015:39-40
[57] Dickie 2015:41. See also Dainotto, 2015, p. 25-26.

carried out an investigation that revealed how the mafia had infiltrated the citrus industry through the development of a *cosca* - or a "family" - based in a nearby village. The leader of this cosca was Antonino Giammona, a man from a peasant family who had earned his fame through the 1848 and 1860 revolutions in which he fought with great courage and rose up the ranks of society, acquiring a great deal of property.[58] At the same time, these revolutions provided the firepower that men like Giammona needed to continue to build a fearsome reputation.[59]

The Giammona family was the first to run protection rackets, using the lemon groves as their territory. They threatened landowners to hire their members in key positions. Thanks to the network they had built - including people at every stage of the process, from cart drivers to wholesalers to dockers - they were able to hinder a farm or ensure its prosperity. From their secure position, they could skim profits off the farm at every stage. Dr. Galati came to learn that he was not the only Giammona's victim, but one of many in what amounted to a strategic campaign. [60]

Dr. Galati took the evidence to higher levels but continued to encounter corruption and face threats. While he decided his own life was not at risk due to his high profile status, his next warden was also shot. Luckily, he was only wounded and able to positively identify his attackers. Dr. Galati cared for the man, but as soon as he was better, he went to Giammona and agreed to drop the charges against his men. [61] Back to where he started, Dr. Galati ended up having to take his family to Naples and go into exile, fully convinced of the veracity of the death-threats by then.[62] From Naples, he sent a letter to Rome in which he reported that in his village of 800 people, there had been twenty-three murders in a single year, including women and children, and ten more that had been seriously wounded.

Despite Dr. Galati's efforts to document and report his encounters with the mafia, the Italian state proved untrustworthy and incompetent. Giammona had powerful friends, and when charges were brought against him, he had a parade of prestigious witnesses testify in his defense. The matter was closed with little more than the promise of increased surveillance. From this ignoble beginning, the mafia would continue to build power and momentum, thanks to the weakness of the newly-formed Italian nation-state.[63]

Dr. Galati's experience should have been an alarm for the Italian government, proving their understanding of the Sicilian mafia as an ancient criminal underworld or transient form of

---

[58] Dickie 2015:44
[59] Dainotto 2015:25
[60] Dickie 2015:44
[61] Dickie 2015:44
[62] Cawthorne 2012
[63] Dickie 2015:44.

political rebellion was incorrect. Instead, a careful reading of his traumatic encounter with the mafia showed that it was actually a kingdom within a kingdom, a diffuse network of power, and an alternative hierarchy that sometimes worked in concert with and sometimes superseded official forms of law and order.[64]

In Dr. Galati's early experience, evidence emerged that the Cosa Nostra has always worked in a complex way, incorporating different structural elements to create its unique, powerful status. First, it is like a shadow state that presumes to hold the power of life and death over its citizens, arbitrarily deciding who deserves to live or die according to its whims. Moreover, it tries to control territory by divvying areas up under the control of different mafia families or coscas. These shadow governments "protect" the people in their territories through rackets that tax all economic activity (whether legal or illegal) through the "*pizzo*," an amount of money that everyone conducting business in the territory must offer.[65] Although Dr. Galati did not realize it, it is likely that his wardens were not actually innocent bystanders but members of a rival cosca.

The Cosa Nostra is also like any illegal business whose goal is to make a profit through scaring potential "associates." It exerts power in a range of markets, such as construction and tobacco, that are profitable and violent, where the mafia's brand of hair-raising aggression can function.

Finally, the Cosa Nostra works like a secret society in that it picks its associates with great care and imposes serious restrictions upon them in exchange for membership. The mafia code is that its members must be subtle, submissive, and above all violent.[66] This similarity to the ancient secret society is visible in the initiation ritual Dr. Galati's investigation brought to light.

Although he failed to make formal headway against the Giammona cosca, Dr. Galati's testimony provides valuable documentation about the Cosa Nostra's earliest stages of development. In addition to the protection rackets he identified, he also gave evidence about the early existence of the literal blood oath used to bind mafiosi, one that is still in use today. In this ritual, a man of honor was presented to a group of bosses, one of whom would prick his arm and tell him to smear it onto a sacred image of Saint Anthony, which they would then burn while reciting an oath. The scattering of the image's ashes was meant to represent the annihilation of all traitors.[67]

Although the ritual seems dramatic and mysterious, Dr. Galati's story works to distill the very essence of the Cosa Nostra into its simplest form. After all, the mafia was not about ancient ideals of honor, nor was it the result of backwardness. Instead, it was a contemporary conflict that pitted the landowners against their guardians over the power to control a lucrative industry.

---

[64] Fentress 2018:7

[65] In this scenario, the Cosa Nostra works to protect parties with conflicting interests, including the owner of a store and the gang of thieves that rob it. Thus, they are the only true beneficiaries (Dickie, 2015, p. 22).

[66] Dickie 2015:21-22

[67] Dickie 2015:45

It was, effectively, a class war that ended up influencing every aspect of Sicilian life.[68]

The earliest attempts at prosecuting the mafia seemed to have ended as soon as they began, but Dr. Galati's documents did, however, make it to Parliament in 1875 and eventually delivered its findings in 1877. The importance of this early inquiry is in the fact that it proves the extent to which the Italian government was aware of the mafia's goings-on from its earliest days, and thus contributed to the consolidation of its power. Because these years were so formative for both the Italian nation and the mafia, a little background of the state of Italian politics will help set the stage on which their intertwined drama played out.

After Italy's unifications, the earliest efforts to govern the country were plagued by difficulties as a series of competing interests had to find a way to form a governable majority. The first coalition, whose main supporters were conservative northern landowners, that ruled Italy in the 15 years after unification was known as the Right. The opposition, an even looser grouping of members mainly tied to South Italy and Sicily, was known as the Left. Due to the weak infrastructure plaguing the south, the Left lobbied for higher government spending, but more than an opposing set of policy ideas, the Left and Right were divided by cultural differences. The Right saw the Parliamentarians of the Left as inferior men who owed their elections to corruption. The Left saw their counterparts on the Right as snobbish, detached, and responsible for the ongoing lack of development in the south. [69]

At the moment of this Parliamentary inquiry in 1874, the Right began to lose its control of the government, primarily because of civic unrest continuing to foment in Sicily due to its dislike of their taxation policy. In the election of 1874, a leading Leftist named Nicolò Colonna began to gain power on the island of Sicily thanks to Giammona's support, and the fact that he controlled 50 of the votes in his district, enough to weigh heavily on the tiny electorate.[70] When the Right barely managed to hang on to power, they lashed out against the Sicilian Left, attacking them as corrupt mafiosi. Beyond mere rhetoric, the government also passed some highly repressive legislation promising to punish anyone associated with criminal activity for up to five years and without trial.

---

[68] Dainotto 2015:27-28

[69] Dickie 2015:69-75

[70] Colonna, who served as a key source for one of the inquiries into the mafia, has long been suspected of being a mafioso because of his relationship to Giammona and his excellent knowledge into the inner workings of the Cosa Nostra. However, there has never been a clear answer to these questions. One hypothesis is that he was the first of many politicians who exchanged votes with the mafia for favors, like government contracts or favorable land zoning. See Dainotto, 2015, p. 34.

Colonna

At that point, statistics seemed to heavily favor the Right's suspicion that something was rotten in the south. Whereas the murder rate for 1873 in northern Lombardy was 1 out of 44,674 inhabitants, in Sicily it was 1 out of every 3,194 inhabitants, a shocking difference.

While this skyrocketing murder rate obviously needed to be addressed by the authorities, the Right did so in a manner serving to inflame all Sicilians, overreaching their mark by effectively targeting not just prominent criminals like Colonna but a majority of Sicilian landowners who were actually victims of the mafia. Furthermore, these policies extinguished all hope within the Sicilian ruling class that they would be able to rely on the national government to free the island of organized crime. Instead, they felt personally attacked.

All of this tension came to a head when a member of the Left, former Sicilian prosecutor Diego Tajani, stood in front of Parliament and accused the Right of being complicit in supporting the development of the mafia following the revolt of 1866, when they rewarded known mafioso for supplying information on political subversives. The Parliament erupted, and Tajani was only able to finish his speech the following day, declaring, "The mafia in Sicily is not dangerous or invincible in itself. It is dangerous and invincible because it is an instrument of local government."

The potential crisis in the Italian government was palpable as a result of these incendiary yet highly credible accusations, and both Left and Right agreed to outsource the matter to a commission of inquiry that would look more generally into Sicilian society. When the nine members of the commission visited the island of Sicily in 1875-1876, they were cordially greeted by the towns and met with local leaders, some of whom barely concealed their mockery of the inquiry. Other leaders and regular citizens provided actual evidence confirming the stranglehold the mafia had on the citrus industry, as had Dr. Galati.

Although the report was not conclusive, it was certainly problematic and well-substantiated. Had the commissioning government been in better health, and had the commissioners themselves been bolder, it would have generated serious alarm. Instead, the report pulled its punches, defining the mafia as a bunch of lowlife criminals who worked against - rather than with - the local government. Even this weakened conclusion did not generate a sufficient response - when the commission brought it to Parliament in 1877, the Right coalition had fallen and the government was in disarray. Thus, the mafia took its first crucial step toward acceptance by the Italian state.[71]

The Murky Origins of the Camorra

The Camorra owes its distinctive features to the Neapolitan metropolitan area in which it sprung up. As the winds of revolution blew through Europe, Naples entered what some have called its "tragic centuries" (which, these same people claim, are not yet over).[72] The tragic centuries started with a rather demoralizing event, when, in the wake of the French Revolution, the people of Naples declared the Parthenopean Republic, an echo of their Greek heritage. They managed to hold their independence for all of five months, from January to June of 1799, before King Ferdinand was able to reclaim the throne.[73]

This brief failed revolution represented just a fragment of time of these so-called tragic centuries, but it is nonetheless emblematic of what was deemed to be a "failed" societal redemption.[74] During this time, Naples appears to suffer an irresolvable paradox. On the one hand, it unquestionably faced economic and political decline, but on the other hand, it also managed to produce a dynamic, engaged intellectual life, including an exceptional artistic, literary, and urban culture that never lost a certain exuberant quality.

---

[71] Dickie 2015:69-75

[72] Pellegrino D'Acierno and Stanislao G. Pugliese, "Preface. The Irresolvable Paradox: Essaying Naples," in *Delirious Naples: A Cultural History of the City of the Sun*, ed. Pellegrino D'Acierno and Stanislao G. Pugliese (New York: Fordham Univ Press, 2018), 1.

[73] Davis, 4.

[74] Davis, 4.

A depiction of Naples during the Parthenopean Republic

In 1806, Napoleon and the French briefly took over, and though Napoleon never visited Naples, the city played an important part in the French imperial system as a source of raw material, money, and human labor. These they provided only in part because the Bourbon rulers and their British allies managed to hold onto Sicily, posing a threat to the French Empire on the mainland.[75]

Nonetheless, the Napoleonic government brought major changes to the city and the kingdom, especially in terms of its social and economic structure. For instance, it immediately struck down the feudal system, and the French also transformed the tax codes, judicial and administrative institutions, and used the French example as their example.[76] According to a writer at the time, the transformations Naples underwent during the Napoleonic period were "convulsions" that knew no parallel in history.[77] However, this period of reform was short-lived; when the French lost the Battle of Waterloo in 1815, control returned to the Spanish Bourbons, and the restoration brought a period of intellectual and cultural stagnation. Naples would suffer civic unrest until Italy was unified under Garibaldi.[78]

Although the French occupation was a blip, its legacy lived on, paradoxically enough,

---

[75] John A. Davis, *Naples and Napoleon: Southern Italy and the European Revolutions, 1780-1860* (OUP Oxford, 2006), 1.

[76] Astarita, 5.

[77] Davis, 2.

[78] Scarth, 3-4; Astarita, 5.

precisely because the reforms failed. According to historians over the past 200 years, the failures of these reforms to take hold provided some of the reasons Southern Italy was never able to embrace Western modernity. They argued that the Napoleonic rule of Naples was their chance to move closer to the political and cultural models of the most "advanced" European nations; having forever missed their chance, the south was now doomed to be backwards forever.[79] This perceived failure, referred to as the "passive revolution" by Vincenzo Cuoco, the city's first historian, continues to haunt Naples to this day.[80]

Meanwhile, the Kingdom of Naples was, until the unification of Italy, the largest territorial state in Italy. Its borders extended from the southern borders of the Lazio (the region of which Rome is the capital) and Marche, all the way to the Strait of Messina in Sicily.[81] Thus, it's no surprise Naples would play a major role in the wars of independence that united Italy.

After the failed First Italian War of Independence, a war against Austria was plotted in 1858, with a territorial agreement drawn up in advance. The confederation of Italian states, to be headed by the pope, would include Piedmont in control of northern Italy (it would give Nice and Savoy to France), a central Italian kingdom around Tuscany, the territory surrounding Rome that would be left to the papacy, and the kingdom of Sicily (and Naples), which would remain the same. They decided to use *agents provacateurs* to stir up a revolt around Modena and then turn to the king for help. The deal almost fell through, as the king did not want to agree to one little detail: allowing his beloved daughter to marry the infamously debauched cousin of Napoleon III.

From the beginning, almost nothing went right. The "revolt" in Italy failed to catch fire, and the only reason war broke out at all is because the Austrians actually decided to flex their military muscle against Piedmont, thinking France would not defend its ally. Hostilities finally broke out in April 1859, but things only got worse when Napoleon III found out Piedmontese Prime Minister Cavour was actually plotting to annex part of the Papal States, betraying the terms of their agreement. Worse, he learned Prussia was planning to get involved in the conflict. As a result, without bothering to consult Cavour, Napoleon III signed an armistice with Austria. Per the terms of this agreement, Austria had to give up control of most of Lombardy to Piedmont,[82] but in exchange they were given the Veneto. The whole debacle was a humiliation for Cavour, who resigned in anger, but he would return to power once again in January 1860.

What the leaders could not have expected was that this manufactured conflict was actually the necessary precursor to Italian unification.[83] The so-called "Second War of Independence" ended

---

[79] Davis, 2.
[80] Davis, 3.
[81] Eleni Sakellariou, *Southern Italy in the Late Middle Ages: Demographic, Institutional and Economic Change in the Kingdom of Naples, c.1440-c.1530* (Leiden and Boston: BRILL, 2011), 9.
[82] Beales and Biagini, introduction.<Should this match 56 below?
[83] Marco Soresina, *Italy Before Italy: Institutions, Conflicts and Political Hopes in the Italian States, 1815-1860* (New York: Routledge Studies in Modern European History, 2018), chapter 7.

up spurring a series of real patriotic uprisings in central Italy, starting in Tuscany and Romagna and then spreading to Umbria. Cavour tried to seize this opportunity to persuade the regions to agree to join with Piedmont, but he was rebuffed. On the balance, the fighting in 1859 did not go as Cavour had planned, but it did have the major advantage of helping him expand Piedmont. The concession of Nice and Savoy to France, however, was seen as a major loss, and even worse, Cavour gave Napoleon III these cities in a secret treaty which he himself believed was unconstitutional. [84]

At the start of 1859, Italy was divided into seven parts, with six sovereign states and one territory (part of Lombardy and Venetia) under the Austrian Empire. The peninsula had not been united since the Roman Empire, but less than two years later, unification would be achieved.[85]

In the years following the unification, the newly formed Italian government primarily focused its attention on the more industrialized north and the new capital of Rome, and it did little to actually help people in the south. In fact, Naples did not enjoy the same demographic boom as other major metropolitan areas in Italy. In the remaining 40 years of the century, it increased by a scant 26%, compared to other Italian cities that grew at double, triple, or quadruple that rate.[86]

Naples shouted for attention, however, when it was hit with a major cholera epidemic.[87] Although its population growth had stagnated, by 1884 Naples was the largest city in Europe. It had a population of almost half a million people, all crammed into an urban center that was a mere eight square kilometers and dealing with living conditions that were staggeringly poor. When public officials tried to bring the epidemic under control, they were caught off guard by how poorly prepared they were. Italy's leading politician at the time, Agostino Depretis, actually argued for gutting the city in a famous declaration that led to a series of protests from southern intellectuals. In the end, the city weathered the epidemic, only to suffer more epidemics in 1910 and 1911.[88]

While the cholera epidemic did nothing to help Naples' reputation, even before the great cholera epidemic actually hit, Naples had already acquired a reputation for its nasty odors and peculiar tasting water, such that tourists often avoided the city. Many northern Europeans believed that Europe ended with Rome and that anything south of Rome was actually Africa.[89] When they did choose to visit Naples, they claimed to stay only long enough to see the required

---

[84] Duggan, 129-30.

[85] Marco Soresina, *Italy Before Italy: Institutions, Conflicts and Political Hopes in the Italian States, 1815-1860* (New York: Routledge Studies in Modern European History, 2018), chapter 7.

[86] Turin grew sixty-three percent during that same period, and Milan grew a whopping one hundred and three percent. Frank M. Snowden, *Naples in the Time of Cholera, 1884-1911* (Cambridge, UK: Cambridge University Press, 2002), 14.

[87] Naples had already been hit by an epidemic in 1837 which killed approximately 14,000 people. Lucy Riall, *The Italian Risorgimento: State, Society and National Unification* (New York: Routledge, 2002), 43.

[88] On the recovery efforts and subsequent crises, see Snowden.

[89] On the British travelers' prejudices against southern Italy, see Ouditt.

ancient sights, and during their stay they would only drink wine and spend most of the time covering their noses.

Of course, the Neapolitans were not ignorant or happy about their city's reputation. One public figure, Alderman Vincenzo Pizzuti, complained in 1873 that the press described the Neapolitans as if they were "semi-barbarian Africans."[90] In an early edition, the famous *Baedeker's* guidebook urges special precautions to English people visiting southern Italy, warning them that they are likely to be cheated financially by the wily people when bargaining for souvenirs, especially if they do not speak any Italian.[91]

Another famous pair of visitors, the renowned German philosopher Walter Benjamin and his companion, Asja Lacis, were more complimentary when they arrived in 1923 and penned a short essay about the experience.[92] They reveled in the city's picturesque elements, with its tradition of Greek costumes and deep-rooted superstitions. They famously described the city as "porous," referring first to the porosity of the volcanic material used in so many buildings in the city. They also used porosity to refer to the blending of cultures that can be found throughout, including Greek, Roman, Byzantine, Arab, Norman, French and Spanish influences. Finally, they mentioned the porosity of life in Naples, as the tight spaces forced bodies into close proximity, and the warm temperatures and poor living conditions pushed much of daily life into the outdoors.[93]

By the end of the 19th century, the city of Naples was a dynamic place with a densely populated center, where people of all social classes lived in extremely close proximity and all kinds of economic activity were conducted in a tiny space. The Camorra, growing up out of a prison system during the era of unification, would be positioned to feed off these vital economic activities, working in legal areas such as agriculture, transportation, construction, clothing and legal gambling. At the same time, from the earliest days they were also involved in illegal activities, such as smuggling, drugs, prostitution, illegal gambling, and money lending.[94]

The Neapolitan Camorra was born in the middle of the 1800s, before the Italian nation had unified itself, during a time of great social tension. At that time, Italy was divided up into different large states and smaller duchies. Naples was the capital of the Kingdom of the Two Sicilies, and it was ruled by the foreign Bourbon dynasty. Fittingly enough, the origin of the Camorra was from within the Bourbon prison system, which was nothing short of inhumane. Because of the costs associated with running a prison, the Bourbons allowed the daily operations

---

[90] Snowden, 11.

[91] Karl Baedeker, *Italy from the Alps to Naples; Handbook for Travellers* (New York City: C. Scribner's sons, 1909), http://archive.org/details/italyfromalpston00karl.

[92] Walter Benjamin and Asja Lacis, "Naples," in *Reflections: Essays, Aphorisms, Autobiographical Writing*, ed. Peter Demetz, trans. Edmund Jephcott (New York: Schocken Books, 1986), 163–73.

[93] On the theoretical significance of porosity, see Serenella Iovino, *Ecocriticism and Italy: Ecology, Resistance, and Liberation* (London: Bloomsbury Publishing, 2016).

[94] Brancaccio, "Violent Contexts and Camorra Clans," 137.

to be guided, in a de facto manner, by the toughest inmates. These inmates started extortion rackets that took advantage of the other inmates as well as the employees, until they were organized enough to become a sworn secret society and to branch out beyond the dungeon.

The story of the rise of the Camorra can be traced back to the fall of Napoleon, who had briefly deposed the Bourbons in 1805 before finally being vanquished in 1815. When the Bourbons were able to return to power, in what was known as the Restoration, they took advantage of some of the reforms the French had started to put into place in order to cement their authority. When a new generation of noble Italian patriots started to resist the reactionary proposals of the Bourbon restoration, they were thrown into jail, including Duke Sigismondo Castromediano.

The numbers of political prisoners increased notably around 1848, when major revolts exploded across the peninsula as part of the First Italian War of Independence. These prisoners were considered an international scandal because of their upper-class backgrounds. When a member of British Parliament, William Ewart Gladstone, visited a prison and witnessed the horrific treatment of the noblemen, he spread the alarm, announcing that the Bourbons had allowed the prisoners to run the jail themselves. In his letter denouncing them, Gladstone used their name, bringing the Camorra out into the open, and threatening that the Austrians deserved to be brought down, because of their shameful conduct.

When the leader of the Italian independence movement, Giuseppe Garibaldi, landed in Messina in 1860, he set off a series of events that would lead to Italian unification in 1861. Among these events was the liberation of the patriotic prisoners of the Kingdom of the Two Sicilies. Finally free, they headed north and took up their position among the new elite of their country. Some would become heroes in the history of the new country, while others had already become villains, choosing to join up with the ranks of the Camorra in prison rather than suffer their relentless harassment. Through it all, as people celebrated the newly founded country, the fact that a criminal organization was gaining momentum was widely overlooked.

One of these prisoners, Castromediano, dedicated his life to the study of the Camorra, whose earliest moments he had witnessed as a prisoner. From his account, historians know about the initial fundraising strategies of the organization, most notable of which was that they levied a tax on every aspect of a prisoner's life, charging him for every bite of food and every scrap of clothing. They had to contribute money to pay for oil for the Madonna's lamp, a tiny altar in most dungeons, and they were forced to pay rent for the tiny piece of floor on which they slept. In this context, the word "pizzo" (prison slang for bribe) was born. Those who refused to pay were punished in a range of ways, from insults to physical aggression, including murder. The authority of the Camorra was so absolute within the walls of the prison that prisoners were not allowed to do anything without its permission, including arguing about any rights they thought they had or complaining to the authorities about poor conditions.

Castromediano also bore witness to the gruesome, yet precise system of capital punishment the Camorra established within the jail system. When someone was marked for death, they held a fake trial in order to legitimize the decision. There was a judge, witnesses, and "lawyers" for both sides. Then, when a judgment had been determined, they made a drawing of the planned murder on the wall of the bathroom before carrying out the execution with cool precision. Everyone in the jail knew what was about to happen, except for the victim. The guiding principle of the Camorra "courts" was not justice, but honor. Indeed, they referred to themselves as the Honored Society.

In addition to levying taxes and operating a judicial system, Castromediano also documented the Camorra's sense of their own statehood. They had complex rules about jurisdiction, the organization of their bureaucratic positions, and the functioning of their administration. Effectively, from his written account, what emerges is that in the earliest days of the prison system, the Camorra was a fully functional shadow state. They even did things like encourage gambling and drinking in order to tax those activities, just like in the outside world. Moreover, they offered lines of credit to the unlucky gamblers and ran the "tavern" that was inside the prison. Anyone who failed to pay would lose whatever objects he had, and then those objects would be resold to others at a huge markup. They were so proud of their abilities to make money in the disgusting dungeon that they became famous for boasting, "We extract gold from fleas."

For the wealthier, the Camorra could make life in prison more comfortable. They could pay for private cells to sleep in, nicer rations, and even access medical care. Only by virtue of the Camorra's blessing could prisoners hope to exchange letters, read books, or purchase candles. Together, they had a smooth double business comprised of taxes and contraband trafficking, the two activities that make up the central pillars of the Camorra today.

Curiously, as Castromediano was transferred between jails during the course of his incarceration, he encountered a variety of mafiosi from different regions, including Sicily and Calabria. They each had their own allegiances and their own dress codes (the Sicilians wore black, while the Neapolitans preferred to show off their wealth by wearing any gold jewelry they could, including on the tassels of the fez hats that they wore). Eventually, the different mafias would go their separate ways and follow their individual industries, but they all shared a common period of overlap in the prisons of Italy before the unification, during which they all referred to themselves as part of the "Honored Society."

Castromediano was eventually freed, but he was unable to win his fortune in the new Italian state. He retired to his dilapidated castle in Puglia and wrote the memoirs that helped illuminate to future historians the shadowy underworld of the mafia.[95]

---

[95] Dickie, *Blood Brotherhood,* 1-14. His unfinished memoirs are published as Sigismondo Castromediano, *Carceri e galere politiche* (Tip. editrice Salentina, 1896).

A Pact with the Patriots

In 1850, around the time that Castromediano was languishing under the thumb of the Camorra in prison, Naples was a large and bustling city. With around 500,000 inhabitants, it was the capital of the Kingdom of the Two Sicilies and the biggest city in Italy. It had the highest population density in all of Europe, and the misery of its poorest inhabitants spilled out onto the streets, spreading everywhere for all to see. There was an infant mortality rate of 30% and a life expectancy in its poorest areas of just 25. Parts of the city were completely outside any official form of law and order, and tourists who came to the city for its famed art and nature were horrified by what they saw. Theft and prostitution were commonplace, and even the children were involved. The best that the police could do was to try to minimize the damage these people caused, and in order to do so they decided to start collaborating with the worst of the thugs to assist in improving law and order.

The grotesque spectacle of Naples also attracted the attention of the upper classes who sought to study the situation with the goal of diagnosing and curing it. Antonio Scialoja, an economist from Naples who had also done time in the Bourbons' jails, was one of those scholars. He wrote against the horrors of prison, recounting many of the same things Duke Castromediano wrote about, but he also discussed rape. Scialoja was able to follow the Camorra activity beyond the walls of the dungeon thanks to his experience as an economist, and he used his knowledge of accounting to figure out that the police had a slush fund that they used to hire spies from amongst the most feared gang members in the city. They even recruited police from among the gang's ranks, putting them openly on the payroll. These men, known as the *feroce* ("ferocious ones"), were not only paid by the police but were also able to supplement their income with bribes. By 1857, there were 181 such men within the police system, and along with the police, they worked to manage crime using the same tactics that the Camorristi had in prison, often because they were the very same people. The men of the dungeons were thus able to get their first foothold on the streets of Naples.

Luckily for them, the tactics that served them so well in prison proved to be perfectly adaptable to the outside world. They started their business by taking cuts of profits from illegal activity, taxing thieves, prostitutes, and gamblers. Soon, however, they were able to move into lawful industries as well. They positioned themselves strategically in places like the ports, the city gates, and the markets, anywhere that money passed through. They soon involved anyone who participated in distribution, from dockworkers to wholesalers to cart drivers, forcing them to pay the protection *pizzo* or risk losing their goods.

In addition to these kinds of money-making schemes, the mafiosi were encouraged by the Bourbon authorities to harass anyone who was agitating politically for Italian unification. One particularly egregious story that Scialoja was able to recount was the story of Aversa Joe, a gentleman prisoner arrested as a patriot after the failed 1848 revolution. Aversa Joe decided to join up with the Camorra and took on a risky job in exchange for having his death sentence commuted: the Neapolitan police were planning to kill off some of the patriots in prison, and they needed a man on the inside. Twice he tried to rally a group of Camorristi to murder their fellow jail mates, but twice he was defeated. The political prisoners wrote to the police authorities to complain and threatened that if the targets were murdered, there would be diplomatic consequences. In response, Aversa Joe was transferred to another prison. Soon after, he was released and hired by the police force. In his story, it is possible to trace a rather chilling trajectory from patriot to Camorrista to corrupt policeman.[96]

The next opportunity for the Camorra to gain increased legitimacy came with the arrival of Garibaldi in Sicily in the summer of 1860. The fact that the Kingdom of the Two Sicilies was being torn apart by the patriot Garibaldi and his army of 1,000 volunteers was deeply disturbing to the Bourbon King Francesco II, who was young and inexperienced. In response to the obvious success that Garbibaldi was having in Sicily, King Francesco II came up with a plan of his own, a pathetic last-ditch attempt to maintain power. On June 26, he proclaimed the "Sovereign Act," which turned the Kingdom of the Two Sicilies from an absolute monarchy to a constitutional monarchy. It announced the formation of a government of liberal patriots, with amnesty for political prisoners and the adoption of the Italian red, white and green flag. This was too little, too late, and everyone was aware of it. The city of Naples braced for what they knew was to come: mass chaos, looting, and pillaging, as regularly happened in these moments of political crisis.

[96] Dickie, *Blood Brotherhood,* 14-20.

King Francesco II

Garibaldi

A clash between the patriots and the loyalists did take place soon after, with two important casualties: the French ambassador and Aversa Joe, who was brutally hacked to death while being transported to the hospital with a minor wound. In the wake of these two murders, the Neapolitan police left their positions in great numbers and a mob overtook the police stations. At this point, the violence did not get any worse, to everyone's great surprise. Instead, as organized gangs started defacing the police stations, the city of Naples appeared strangely calm. There was none of the typical looting, just the burning of policemen's possessions that were found in the stations.

This uncharacteristic takeover of the police stations was directed by Liborio Romano, a patriot who had been jailed in the early 1850s before being released because of his severe health problems. In exchange, he signed an oath of loyalty to the Bourbon monarchy and, in 1860, agreed to take up a position as the head of the new police force. Romano had quite the approach to handling his duty: he immediately invited the Camorra to "rehabilitate itself" by essentially becoming the police force. Naturally, the leading bosses were only too excited to jump at the chance. Romano was revered in Naples, and the rest of Italy looked to his proposal as a model for their own recruitment policies, allowing Camorristi to join the new National Guard. It was a rare occasion in which the elitist northern Italians looked to the southerners as a model for government policy.[97]

More information about the extent of the entrenchment of the Camorra in the politics of Italy around the time of the unification emerged through the account of Swiss writer Marc Monnier, who ran a hotel in Naples. Thanks to his ideal positioning within this hub of travelers, Monnier was able to get unparalleled information about how the Camorra exerted its control on the territory, including demanding the *pizzo* from the porters, shopkeepers, and carriage drivers, and collecting taxes from the street card players. From his position as an outsider with keen insider knowledge, Monnier wrote a book that includes vital testimony from a number of different kinds of witnesses, including a patriot who was part of a group called the "Committee of Order." Intentionally the opposite of what their name promised, this group wanted to foment unrest in order to over throw the Bourbons, and they made their own pact with the Camorra to further that goal.

From this testimony, it becomes clear how complex and contradictory the relationship was between patriots and the Camorra, as their affiliation encompassed everything from outright hate and persecution to collaboration. Indeed, in the uncertain times leading up to unification, the patriots tried every approach they thought possible in order to reach their goals. They knew that the Bourbon police often turned to the Camorra for help, and some of their ranks decided it would be in the best interest of the *patria* (the Italian nation) to compete with the authorities for the loyalty of the Camorra. In order to secure this loyalty, the patriots agreed to pay a number of Camorra bosses a huge sum of money with the goal of bringing down the Bourbon state: 10,000 ducats each (or what would today be approximately $170,000). They claimed this money was to help them prepare for the revolution, although it appears that all they did was print inspirational signs and pocket the rest of the money. They continued to extort further payments, threatening to reveal the plot to the Bourbons unless more money was forked over to fill their coffers.

However unfaithful the Camorra might have been in the earlier years, by 1859, when the Bourbon police started to turn on them, the Camorra bosses decided to make good on their promise. They understood that the patriots might have more to offer them than just money. Thanks to the years of extortion and negotiation, when the Bourbon police forces collapsed, the Camorra was standing at the ready to take power, which explains the strange calm that settled over the streets of Naples during a moment that should have been explosive.

It is unclear why Liborio Romano made the deal that he did. Monnier believed it had to do with Monnier's belief in the secret society Freemason patriotic ideals, and his hope that the Camorra bosses would help realize the project of Italy. Others have speculated that he did so out of fear, as the bosses (quite probably) threatened anarchy on the streets or may have even threatened to

---

[97] Dickie, *Blood Brotherhoods*, 20–26. For Monnier's book see, Marc Monnier, *La camorra: notizie storiche* (G. Barbèra, 1863).

kill him if he did not comply. Still others have asserted that he did it out of personal and professional interest, not because he was being coerced.

When Garibaldi reached Naples in September 1860, the Camorra was able to cash in on its investment with the patriots. Thanks to their control of the police force, this meant getting their claws even deeper into their business of taxation, as they set up roadblocks that threatened to inhibit all commerce that was not approved by them. They were also well positioned to scoop up the new positions that were being distributed by Garibaldi's government as the Bourbon administration crumbled. Thanks to their shameless behavior and their deeply entrenched connections, they were able to wheedle their way into other government offices and secure other choice positions for their friends and associates.

In October 1860, the city of Naples voted in resoundingly definitive numbers to enter the Kingdom of Italy, and now that Naples was a part of Italy, the transitional government of Garibaldi gave way to a new government. The most difficult position went to a man named Silvio Spaventa (ironically, his last name means "he frightens"). Spaventa was another Italian patriot who had cut his teeth in the jails of Bourbon Naples, but the experience had not corrupted him; in fact, it had only made him more steadfast. Unlike the average prisoner, Spaventa used his time in jail to read philosophy, and when he was appointed to the thankless task of reforming the Neapolitan police, he tried to use the abstract lessons he had acquired to do the job.

Spaventa

Spaventa faced unenviable conditions, as Italy in late 1860 was highly unstable. Although Garibaldi had willingly given up control of his territory to the Piedmontese in the north, his followers did not unanimously accept this decision, and many were armed and disgruntled, roaming about the Campanian countryside looking for something to do. Others were hoping that their contributions to the patriotic cause would pay off financially and were frustrated as the free market in Southern Italy got off to a rocky start.

Despite these daunting conditions, Spaventa made an honest effort to fight the Camorra, with mass arrests made in November of that year. Unfortunately, putting the Camorra bosses back in jail, a realm that they knew how to navigate with aplomb, did nothing to curtail their power. The men still on the outside even managed to stage an assault on the prison in order to attempt to free their bosses.

For all his undaunted courage, Spaventa received no adoration from the Neapolitan people, who mistrusted him despite the fact that he was also from the south. To them, he seemed like one of the haughty northern politicians sent down from Turin to control them. There were street demonstrations against him, and eventually there was even a petition for his removal.

Spaventa is important to the history of the Camorra because he was also one of the first people to conduct an official investigation into its mode of operation, which he did along with his friend Marc Monnier. In April 1861, he was ordered to investigate its development from the prisons into general society to answer questions about exactly how it grew into the force it was. What Spaventa uncovered was that the Camorra was divided into 12 chapters that corresponded with the city's 12 quarters, and its main power was concentrated in the four quarters of the impoverished low city. Each chapter had a boss, and each boss was elected by his peers. Alongside the boss was a bookkeeper who had the job of gathering and distributing funds.

In order to be inducted into the Camorra, men had to meet a certain number of criteria. The Camorra had a ban on homosexuals, and it banned anyone who had a prostitute in their family (although this rule was more for show than for actual enforcing). In order to be initiated, the men had to undergo a test, which might involve a murder or simply slashing the face of an enemy (during this time, scars on the face were incredibly common in the poorest areas of Naples).

After meeting the criteria, the initiate had to partake in the ritual that consisted of swearing an oath over crossed knives and engaging in a duel with another member of the Camorra. In order to ascend up the ranks, members of the Camorra had to submit themselves to further knife contests. Knife-fighting was a prized skill for the Camorra, and members practiced extensively, even though the practice was more ceremonial than violent.

The early report from Spaventa and Monnier also identified characteristics that hold true for the Camorra today. For example, the fluid nature of the organization was noted from the beginning. Monnier explained the fluidity of the Camorra in terms of the illiteracy of the members - since they could not read or write, they could not produce written laws, which meant they handed down traditions and established ranks orally. As fluid as it was, however, there was still an overall hierarchy, with the upper ranks shamelessly exploiting the lower ranks and putting them in humiliating and dangerous situations according to their whim. The junior members were often made to take the fall for any crime that a boss was accused of, and if they took the jail sentence, there was a better chance they would be able to become a Camorrista boss upon their release.

Spaventa and Monnier were also left with a major mystery about the origins of the Camorra. The very fact that it is so difficult to figure out the origins of the Camorra is itself significant, as it underscores the popular origins of the phenomenon. Since it emerged from the poorest sectors of society, amongst people with low rates of literacy, it should not be surprising that there is no formal documentation for the early history of this organization.[98] Furthermore, Spaventa and

Monnier had to cope with the fact that the Bourbons had burned the police archives that would have given them the relevant information.[99]

Without all the necessary information, they speculated that the Spanish were responsible for the rise of the Camorra, bringing it to the city of Naples during the 16th century. Although there was very little substantive evidence to support this claim, the fact that it was advanced by two serious men in this early report, and the fact that opposing evidence did not emerge until recently, implies that this theory was widely accepted. The evidence they cited included the fact that the word "Camorra" means "fight" in Spanish. Moreover, the famous Spanish author Miguel de Cervantes wrote a short story in 1613 that depicted a criminal organization resembling the mafia.[100] On top of that, they believed there was a secret society in the early 1400s in Spain, although there is no record of it until 1845 and this may have been the product of a popular French novel, inspired by Cervantes and translated into Italian in 1847.[101] The fourth piece of "evidence" was more a prejudice than anything else: the authors believed that Spanish rule in Naples was corrupt. However, the Spanish left Naples in 1707, and there is absolutely no sign of the Camorra for more than 100 years after that, which makes the theory that much less likely to be true.[102]

Although today scholars know that there is no basis to it, the widespread belief in the Spanish theory is itself an interesting part of the history of the Camorra. After all, blaming the Camorra on the Spanish was undoubtedly a convenient tactic that enabled the patriots to distance themselves from the organization and hide the crucial role they had played in creating a sort of shadow state.

Even as Monnier spread the incorrect theory about the Spanish origins of the Camorra, he also gave a number of accurate descriptions about the true nature of its origins, in particular its close association with the Freemason secret societies that had been a popular form of resistance during the 19th century. Closely associated with the French during the brief Napoleonic rule of Naples, the Bourbons banned these secret societies when they returned to power. One particularly powerful sect, the *Carbonari* ("Charcoal Burners"), helped inspire an unsuccessful revolution in Naples in 1820. Despite their lack of success, the *Carbonari* included in its ranks some of the most important men of 19th century Italy, including one of the fathers of Italian unification, Giuseppe Mazzini, and, curiously enough, Liborio Romano. The closely intertwined history of the secret societies and the Camorra are visible in the shared vocabulary between them. The

---

[98] Tom Behan, *See Naples and Die: The Camorra and Organized Crime* (London ; New York: Tauris Parke Paperbacks, 2002), 19.

[99] Francesco Barbagallo, *Storia della camorra* (Gius.Laterza & Figli Spa, 2014).

[100] Miguel De Cervantes, *Rinconete and Cortadillo* (CreateSpace Independent Publishing Platform, 2016).

[101] Alonso de Castillo Solórzano, *La garduña de Sevilla, y anzuelo de las bolsas* (Imprenta de la Viuda de Jordan é Hijos, 1844).

[102] Dickie, *Blood Brotherhood,* 30 – 40.

Camorra referred to its local chapters as "lodges," and the members of the society were part of their "nation."

Spaventa continued his crackdown on the Camorra, but his unpopularity grew to the point that there were attempts on his life. Eventually, he hired some bodyguards who were affiliated with the Camorra themselves, and they brutally murdered one of Spaventa's chief adversaries. Spaventa ended up resigning under a cloud of scandal, and it was a rather ominous sign that this seemingly incorruptible man had also resorted to "co-managing" Naples with his enemies. This pattern would repeat itself throughout the Camorra's history, as the police would swing between repressing the Camorra and working with it.

By the time Spaventa had resigned, the Camorra was actively engaged in national politics, approving which candidates could be elected and following their every move once they entered office. They were able to partner their objectives with those of the politicians, to their mutual benefit.[103]

The first group of politicians to lead Italy in the aftermath of unification was a coalition whose members banded together loosely under the label of the "Right." Not surprisingly, these were wealthy men, most of whom owned land and sought to protect their interests. In the early days of the Italian nation, voting was not a right for all, but only came with property ownership (amounting to two percent of the population), a law that was only changed in 1882. These politicians were also deeply connected to the Savoy monarchy, which was rooted in the region of Piedmont in the north. They had a few southern allies, men like Silvio Spaventa, who shared their values, and the Right believed that they had to fight against the mafia, as it posed an existential threat to the very existence of their fragile nation. Even after Spaventa had to resign, the Right continued to support large-scale roundups of Camorristi in the early years of the new nation. They brought Spaventa aboard the national government, making him a minister and allowing him to continue his investigations. Around the same time, Monnier's book was published, publicizing the problems.

Thanks to Spaventa's collaboration with the government of the Right, Italy established a Parliamentary Commission of Inquiry in order to address the problems of law and order in the south. As a result, they passed a law in August 1863 that allowed certain government officials to punish certain kinds of suspects without a trial. Essentially, it meant that people who were suspected of being mafiosi were allowed to be sent into exile in a penal colony on a desolate island off the coast of Italy. This kind of punishment was thought to be the best way to deal with the Camorristi, who were notoriously slippery. It was assumed that, from an isolated island, they would not be able to go about interfering with judicial processes by intimidating witnesses and corrupting officials.

---

[103] Dickie, *Blood Brotherhood*, 41 – 45.

Once again, however, the Camorra got the better of the government. All these exiled bosses did was effectively repurpose the same strategies that they had used in prison. In the end, Spaventa did nothing to solve the crisis of organized crime in Italy – he inadvertently transferred it to new geographical locations.[104]

What is the 'Ndrangheta?

No one is sure when the name 'Ndrangheta was formally adopted by the Calabrian mafia, but many historians believe it dates to the mid-1950s or early 1960s. It has also been known as the *Onorata Società* ("Honored Society"), the Montalbano Family, *picciotteria*, *maffia*, and *camorra* (the same name as the Neapolitan mafia).)[105] The word itself is thought to mean "manliness" or "courage" in the local dialect of Calabria,[106] and according to two major scholars, the word is Greek in origin. The Greek word *andranghateia* means "society of men of honor," and *andragnatho* means "to engage in military actions." These potential Greek origins are highly plausible in Calabria, given that the region used to be part of Magna Grecia. They cite linguistic evidence to maintain that variants of the word were found in police documents as early as the 1920s, and one scholar suggests it can be dated to 1909.[107] Regardless, at that early date the term did not likely have the same cohesive meaning it acquired in the 1950s.[108]

Just as the Cosa Nostra developed in the Sicilian capital region of Palermo, the 'Ndrangheta had its stronghold in the province of Reggio Calabria and the surrounding countryside. Today Calabria is a region of contrasts, home to both some of the poorest of Italy's citizens and some of its richest, though the latter can be credited in large part to the 'Ndrangheta's leading role in the European cocaine market, which they were able to enter through South American producer cartels.[109] This uneven development is visible throughout Calabria's history, and it certainly helps explain the birth of the 'Ndrangheta in the first place.

Home to less than two million people according to statistics from 2011, Calabria is demonstrably behind the other Italian regions, with a mediocre productivity rate (48.8% compared to 62.2% nationally,) and an above average rate of unemployment (12.7% compared to the national average of 8.4%).[110] As a profoundly fragmented region in terms of its culture, geography, and demographics, Calabria is also highly heterogeneous, with uneven industrialization across its territory. In fact, people sometimes refer to Calabria in the plural, as

---

[104] Dickie, *Blood Brotherhood,* 40 – 46.

[105] Ciconte, "Origins and Development of the 'Ndrangheta."

[106] Dickie, *Blood Brotherhoods,* xxx.

[107] Varese, *Mafias on the Move, How Organized Crime Conquers New Territories*, 31.

[108] John Dickie, *Blood Brotherhoods: A History of Italy's Three Mafias* (PublicAffairs, 2014), 125. Enzo Ciconte claims, instead, that the term *'Ndrangheta* came into its modern usage in the 1960s. Ciconte, "Origins and Development of the 'Ndrangheta."

[109] Dickie, *Blood Brotherhoods,* xxxiii.

[110] Anna Sergi, "The Evolution of the Australian 'Ndrangheta. An Historical Perspective," *Australian and New Zealand Journal of Criminology 2015* 48 (2014): 2.

Calabrie.[111]

This uneven development meant that there was a great deal of suffering among the lower classes, together with a lack of faith in the governing authorities, a characteristic it shared with the other southern Italian regions where mafias also developed. In response, the Calabrian mafiosi were able to present themselves as benefactors for these downtrodden people, showing themselves capable of responding to local needs in a way that the "real" authorities were unable to match.[112]

At the core of the 'Ndrangheta is the family unit, much like in the other Italian mafia organizations. The males in the family comprise the 'ndrina, providing a bond of blood that helps to guarantee a pact of secrecy amongst them. In contrast to the Neapolitan Camorra, which is more diverse and horizontally structured, the 'Ndrangheta is homogenous and hierarchical, with detailed written rules and formal procedures for governance. Thanks to this tightly controlled structure, of the three main Italian mafias, the 'Ndrangheta is the most famous for the cult of silence and secrecy, known as *omertà.* Remarkably, even elementary schoolchildren in Calabria adhere to this principle - when one journalist asked local kids whether they had ever heard of the 'Ndrangheta, they denied it and said that what happens outside of school is not their concern.[113]

This strong belief in *omertà* is why it is relatively rare for mafiosi to betray their fellow members and become cooperating witnesses if they get caught, and since the 'Ndrangheta can boast the fewest collaborators with the government (known as *pentiti*), it has been particularly hard to prosecute. As of 1995, the 'Ndrangheta had 133 pentiti out of a 5,000 person membership, a rate of 2.6%, compared to the slightly higher rate of 2.8% of the Camorra and much higher rate of 6.9% for the Cosa Nostra.[114] For example, there had never been a *pentito* in the town of Careri despite having 600-700 *picciotti* (the plural of *picciotto,* which means young boy in the southern Italian dialect) out of a population of a few thousand. It was not until 2006 that the organization had its first *pentito* ever, and his entire family disowned him.[115] In another case, from July 2010, 300 men were arrested by Italian law enforcement and charged with affiliation with the 'Ndrangheta, in a mission known as Operation Crime. True to the code of *omertà,* however, most of the men have refused to cooperate.[116]

Beyond the mafiosi's deep belief in honor and in family ties, there is a more venal reason why of the few *pentiti* who come forward, few of them actually end up cooperating with the state.

---

[111] Sergi and Lavorgna, *'Ndrangheta,* 4.
[112] Ercole Giap Parini, "'Ndrangheta. Multilevel Criminal System of Power and Economic Accumulation," in *The 'Ndrangheta and Sacra Corona Unita: The History, Organization and Operations of Two Unknown Mafia Groups,* ed. Nicoletta Serenata, Studies of Organized Crime (Cham: Springer International Publishing, 2014), 51–62, https://doi.org/10.1007/978-3-319-04930-4_4.
[113] Claudio Antonelli and Gianluigi Nuzzi, *Blood Ties: The Calabrian Mafia* (Pan Macmillan, 2012).
[114] Varese, *Mafias on the Move, How Organized Crime Conquers New Territories,* 32.
[115] Antonelli and Nuzzi, *Blood Ties.*
[116] Dickie, *Blood Brotherhood,* xliii - xliv.

Thanks to its vast wealth, the 'Ndrangheta is able to pay off state's witnesses, offering them significantly more money than the state can provide. Moreover, once someone actually does testify against the 'Ndrangheta, their family members become the target of violent aggressions which could explain why the family from Careri disowned their relative with such vehemence.[117]

Thanks to its start in Calabria, today its cells are known as 'ndrina's (possibly derived from the word *malandrina*, meaning "gangster prison cell").[118] As with the other Italian mafias, the 'Ndrangheta is an organization that is based on ties of kinship, and each family unit is at the heart of a larger clan. The boss of the 'ndrina is known as the *capobastone* ("chief cudgel"), and he usually is the father of a number of boys whom he brings into his clan. The clans use marriage alliances to strategically partner up with another. Above the *capobastone* is the *capo locale* ("local boss"), who supervises a number of 'ndrina. He has a number of people supporting him, including a bookkeeper who does all of the accounting and a *capocrimine* ("head of crime"), who keeps a watch out on the territory. When war breaks out with rivals, this *capocrimine* becomes the point man for strategy.

A single *locale* is usually divided into two units and kept in isolation, in order to prevent a major, simultaneous takedown. These two units are also organized hierarchically, with the more prestigious members grouped together.

In order to move up a rank, a member has to earn "flowers." He gets these with every crime he commits, whether theft, extortion, or murder. With every flower, there is another ceremony and, accordingly, more power and information. In recent years, there has apparently been a proliferation of flowers, as the 'Ndranghetisti use these new levels of honor in order to quickly resolve tensions and disputes. All the while, it creates more confusion within the ranks about which member is actually higher.[119]

While some scholars have focused on the structure of the 'Ndrangheta, others have preferred to study the organization in terms of its behavioral model, which they call 'ndranghetism. These scholars believe that the success of the 'Ndrangheta is due to the members' ability to use violence, intimidation, and aggression in order to manipulate social networks and relationships, and to influence traditions, rituals and social practices amongst members of their society. They are able to do this because of their shared values and behaviors, many of which are not criminal at all. For example, marriage traditions are an essential part of 'ndranghetism and becomes a way to monitor the shifting family dynamics.[120] In this system, a woman from one clan is often forced

---

[117] Renate Siebert, "Mafia Women: The Affirmation of a Female Pseudo-Subject. The Case of the 'Ndrangheta," in *Women and the Mafia*, ed. Giovanni Fiandaca, STUDIES IN ORGANIZED CRIME (New York, NY: Springer New York, 2007), 27, https://doi.org/10.1007/978-0-387-36542-8_3.

[118] Another possible meaning for the word 'Ndrina is "man who does not bend," Varese, *Mafias on the Move, How Organized Crime Conquers New Territories*, 31.

[119] Dickie, *Blood Brotherhood*, xliii - xlix.

[120] Sergi and Lavorgna, *'Ndrangheta*, 3.

to marry a man from another clan, with which her male relatives wish to forge an alliance. Then, the more male children she has, the more she is valued, as it is fully expected that her sons will be incorporated into the clan and become its youngest foot soldiers.[121]

As problematic as these behaviors are, it is important to bear in mind that 'ndranghetism can only flourish because of the way Calabrian society is structured. Since there is a weak political class coupled with ample opportunity to start new business ventures, individuals who choose to participate in 'ndranghetism are able to prosper relatively unfettered.[122]

Today, an 'ndrinas can be found not just in Calabria, but also in Rome and throughout the north of Italy, in prosperous regions such as Piedmont, Liguria, Lombardy and Friuli Venezia Giulia. The 'Ndrangheta has also been highly effective in developing cells on every inhabited continent, apart from Asia,[123] and due to the high value it placed on secrecy in the early days, it was able to stay in the shadows, learn important lessons, and put its structures into place before it was widely noticed across the world. Thus, while it is not the oldest of the major Italian mafias, it has been the most efficient on the path to success.[124] It is believed to have taken advantage of mass Calabrian migrations to obtain powerful holdings in Europe (including Belgium, France, Germany, Great Britain, Morocco, Portugal, The Netherlands, Spain, Switzerland and Turkey), as well as North and South America (Argentina, Bolivia, Brazil, Canada,[125] Chile, Colombia, the Dominican Republic, Ecuador, the United States and Venezuela), and even Australia.

It is precisely this ability to spread its cells far and wide by effectively replicating the original organizational structure that makes the 'Ndrangheta so powerful. Those who have studied the transnational nature of the 'Ndrangheta mention that they successfully incorporated a "global" dimension to their activities by using the same shared social and cultural values that they adopted in Calabria in their ventures in foreign countries.[126] While keeping a close association between the motherland and the colonies, they develop a business structure that is simple in its essence: the 'Ndrangheta positions a group of affiliates in legal businesses, and because they are kept at a distance from the illegal activities, these mafiosi actually manage to facilitate them. One common example is that the seemingly legal ventures provide a cover for money laundering and drug smuggling.[127]

---

[121] Ciconte, "Origins and Development of the 'Ndrangheta."

[122] Sergi and Lavorgna, 'Ndrangheta, 3.

[123] Dickie, *Blood Brotherhoods*, xxxiv.

[124] Dickie, *Blood Brotherhoods*, xxxiv.

[125] For more on the 'Ndrangheta in Canada, see Anna Sergi, "What's in a Name? Shifting Identities of Traditional Organized Crime in Canada in the Transnational Fight against the Calabrian 'Ndrangheta," *Canadian Journal of Criminology and Criminal Justice* 60, no. 4 (November 10, 2018): 427–54.

[126] Vincent C. Figliomeni, *'Ndrangheta of Calabria: Exploring a Pragmatic Approach to Confronting ... -* (Bloomington, IN: Author House, 2019), https://books.google.com/books?id=aCugDwAAQBAJ&printsec=frontcover&dq=ndrangheta&hl=en&sa=X&ved=0ahUKEwjwmJL8677jAhXCWc0KHcuICugQ6AEIOzAD#v=onepage&q&f=false.

[127] Nicoletta Serenata, "Introduction," in *The 'Ndrangheta and Sacra Corona Unita: The History, Organization and Operations of Two Unknown Mafia Groups*, ed. Serenata, Nicoletta (New York: Springer, 2014), 1–13.

This homogenous structure is paired with an ability to diversify its businesses, from kidnapping to investments in various sectors, which allows the 'Ndrangheta to be a dynamic, flexible organization. In addition to keeping up with the times, this allows the organization to thrive, and it has even been referred to as the "McDonald's of Mafias."[128] Today, the 'Ndrangheta is believed to be involved in economic and entrepreneurial activities in sectors including rural development, health, tourism, online gambling, soccer,[129] waste disposal, the food industry, transportation, and, ironically, environmental protection. It is able to achieve such diversity because of the emphasis the 'Ndrangheta has put on educating its members, allowing the organization to put on a respectable front by including doctors, lawyers, politicians and engineers. Perhaps more than any other mafia, the 'Ndrangheta has excelled in creating, inhabiting, and expanding a legal gray area where it becomes increasingly difficult to distinguish between legal and illegal activities. This creates major challenges for prosecutors when there are cases to be tried.[130]

Another major distinction between the 'Ndrangheta and other mafias like the Sicilian Cosa Nostra is the fact that the 'Ndrangheta is completely centralized. Despite having countless international branches, every part of the 'Ndrangheta reports back to the headquarters in Italy, known as the *Provincia* ("Province"). The *Provincia* is in charge of distributing power amongst its various colonies, ensuring that nothing happens without its approval.[131]

Once centralized aspect of the 'Ndrangheta is the importance of rituals. This is a quality it once shared with the other two Italian mafias, but while the others have relaxed the attachment to rituals in recent decades, the 'Ndrangheta has intensified its commitment to them. Even in the earliest days, archival papers testify to the fact that the Calabrian mafia was already forming itself into a highly structured organization, with specific jobs assigned to members according to their rank.

One of the most important rituals of the Calabrian mafia is the initiation, during which the members take blood oaths and become blood brothers, after which they are required to spill the blood of their enemies. This bloody symbolism carries them through life together and ends only with death. The bond of the mafioso is exclusively between men, yet women become involved through marriage, where another ritual (the shedding of virginal blood) is the centerpiece.[132] According to one autobiography from a Calabrian who turned himself in to the police, his initiation into the 'Ndrangheta began just after birth, and as the firstborn, the fact that he was a boy was particularly celebrated. His father shot a burst of machine gun bullets up into the sky before taking the newborn to the other members of the clan to introduce him. There, they

---

[128] Luca Rinaldi, "How the 'Ndrangheta Quietly Became the McDonald's of Mafias," *Vice* (blog), April 17, 2014, https://www.vice.com/en_uk/article/9bz3ny/ndrangheta-mafia-italy-calabria-mcdonalds-drugs.

[129] Alberto Testa and Anna Sergi, *Corruption, Mafia Power and Italian Soccer* (Routledge, 2018).

[130] Serenata, "Introduction."

[131] Serenata.

[132] Dickie, *Blood Brotherhoods*, xxxv.

performed the first ritual of a young mafioso's life: they laid him out on a bed with a knife and key on either side of him. As he flailed his arms, they watched to see which he touched. If he touched the key, it meant he was destined to become a member of law enforcement who would lock people up. If it was the knife, he would become a mafioso who would live and die by their code of honor. He did touch the knife first, but, according to the story, that was because some adult had nudged it closer to his tiny hand. He was christened Antonio after his grandfather and destined to become a mafioso like his father. He was officially considered "half in and half out," on the path to becoming a member, but not a full one, which could not come until he could at least walk and talk.[133]

Since he was the son of a boss, Antonio did not have to do much to pass his apprenticeship. He just needed to act as a messenger in order to pass a few secret messages and be responsible for hiding a few weapons. Then, in order to prepare for his induction, he was instructed to memorize a few pages of the official rulebook. He also had to learn the myth of the foundation of the 'Ndrangheta, the story of Osso, Mastrosso and Carcagnosso (discussed below).[134] Then he was allowed to undergo the initiation rite, the most elaborate of any of the Italian mafias, dating from the late 19th century. Brought into a dark room with the senior members present in a circle, he sat silently before them until a series of prayers were said and promises were made. Antonio had to answer three times that he was ready for membership, and then the boss cut a cross onto his left thumb and dripped blood from the wound onto a small picture of the Archangel Michael. They then ripped off the head of the Archangel and burned the rest in the fire, in order to represent the annihilation of all traitors. Then Antonio was invited to take the oath, during which he swore loyalty until his death, pledging even to give his own life if necessary. With another prayer, Antonio's baptism was complete.[135]

The Mythological and Actual Origins of the 'Ndrangheta

The three main Italian mafias all emerged from Italy's south, a territory that was governed primarily by the Spanish Bourbons as the largest region before Italian unification. This region was known as the Kingdom of the Two Sicilies, and thanks to this shared governance under the Spanish Bourbons, the mafias also share a common origin story that begins with the important legend of Osso, Mastrosso, and Carcagnosso. More than a legend, these three mythological figures have inspired thousands of potential mafiosi across the south of Italy.

Today, historians make clear that these individuals never existed, but according to the story, these three men are thought to have been young Spanish knights who were part of a secret society in Toledo named *Garduña*, and who landed in Italy around the year 1412. These three men were not traveling for pleasure, nor for colonial purposes; instead, they were effectively in

---

[133] Dickie, *Blood Brotherhoods,* xxxv-xxxvi.
[134] See Dickie, Blood Brotherhoods, xxv.
[135] Dickie, *Blood Brotherhoods,* xxxviii - xxxix.

exile, fleeing their native land because they dared to defend the honor of their own family by murdering someone who had wronged their sister.

Their first port of arrival was the small island off the western coast of Sicily known as Favignana, where they stayed for 29 years. During this time, they stayed hidden from everybody while they worked underground in the island's network of caves, busily preparing the social rules for what would become the mafia. After this long period of gestation, the three brothers parted ways. Osso went to Sicily and gave birth to the Cosa Nostra, Mastrosso went to Campania to start the Camorra, and Carcagnosso went to Calabria to start up the 'Ndrangheta.

Each one of these figures is assigned a religious identity in the legend of the 'Ndrangheta. Osso represents Jesus Christ, Mastrosso represents Saint Michael the Archangel, and Carcagnosso represents Saint Peter. Others associate each man with patron saints: Saint George belongs to Osso; the Virgin Mary belongs to Mastrosso; and Saint Michael the Archangel or the Archangel Gabriel works to protect Carcagnosso. According to John Dickie, in an early trial of the *picciotti*, a boy testified to the origin story, giving a slightly different version in which each of the knights came from a different region (Spain, Palermo, and Naples) and formed a metaphorical tree with branches, leaves, and flowers that represented the different levels of the members. The *picciotti* were the flowers, a form of symbolism that would recur throughout the 'Ndrangheta's history.[136]

This fairytale (which had been wholly unknown to the actual residents of Favignana who supposedly hosted the men) has played a key role in the development of the culture and ideology of the Calabrian 'Ndrangheta and for their aspiring mafiosi. The symbolism is highly effective, particularly the shared Spanish origins, as well as the themes of revenge, honor, family, secrecy, and rules. Even the island of Favignana, the location of an infamous Bourbon penitentiary, is not a casual choice. Another telling element of the story is the way in which it incorporates sacred iconography together with the profane, so even though mafias are criminal organizations, they are nonetheless deeply tied to Catholicism and often look to religious motifs and history to justify their actions. Thus, the story is the ideal founding myth to inspire the creation of new Mafiosi, who are forced to memorize it as part of their baptism.[137]

The most famous geographical feature of the region of Calabria is Aspromonte, a mountain whose name translates to "harsh mountain." Baked in the sun and hostile to the people and plants trying to live on its slopes, Aspromonte is at once striking and forbidding. Rockslides have been known to wipe out villages and massive earthquakes are a regular occurrence. It is believed that 50,000 people were killed in the 1783 earthquake, and a series of lethal quakes took place with startling frequency at the turn of the 19th century.

---

[136] Dickie, *Blood Brotherhoods,* 125.
[137] Ciconte, "Origins and Development of the 'Ndrangheta."

Marcus Calabresus' picture of Aspromonte

Calabria was never shown the love that most of the Italian peninsula elicited. In fact, as the Grand Tour was sending northern Europeans to Italy in droves, the most famous travel guide of the time told visitors to skip Calabria because of the poor accommodations and uncertain travel conditions they would face. To wit, there was no railway leading travelers to Calabria, as it stopped at the city of Eboli, far to the north of Calabria's northern border. At the time of the unification of Italy, the only way to get to the capital city of Reggio Calabria was to secure one of only three spaces available in the coach that traveled from Eboli. Even aside from problems with roads, weather, or outlaws, the trip would take more than three whole days.

If a traveler made it all the way to Calabria, he would find a population that was 87% illiterate. Peasants were being exploited by their often-absentee landlords, creating a society of extreme disparity between the rich and poor, and the government was poorly run, with mayors and their relatives taking public land for themselves or even engaging in outright theft. Laws could not be enforced, or at least ones that the armed bandits did not approve of. At the same time, however, the early visitors to Calabria would not have noticed any disturbing signs of organized crime, as they would have found in Naples and in Sicily. In the 1860s and 1870s, in fact, there were no signs at all – written or otherwise – that suggest the development of a Calabrian mafia was taking place.

By the 1880s, life in Calabria had started to improve thanks to the introduction of a single-track railway that made its way down the Ionian coast all the way to Reggio Calabria. Perhaps not coincidentally, however, with this improvement in its economic fortunes, the first signs of criminal activity seemed to start springing up from nowhere. In these earliest accounts, historians find words such as mafioso and *camorrista* to describe the gangsters, terms borrowed from the Sicilian and Neapolitan mafias, but it would not be long before the Calabrian gangsters started to get their own terminology. They began to commonly use *picciotto*, a word that had also been used to disparagingly refer to the low-ranking members of the Camorra and may refer to the arrogant, irresponsible attitudes common to young men who lacked real world experience. Roughly translated to mean "boys with attitude," these gangsters came from the lowest rungs of society and had relatively meager ambitions. They simply wanted slightly better living conditions for themselves, some wine to drink, and some meat to eat.

When they first emerged, the *picciotti* faced a number of serious challenges to their authority. In fact, compared to the other two mafias, they were the most seriously prosecuted, emblematic of their low-class status. In the first seven years of their existence, 1,854 *picciotti* were tried and sentenced to prison. The government was not on their side, as they had not managed to infiltrate law enforcement to the extent their Sicilian and Neapolitan counterparts had. However, even if they were prosecuted within Calabria, the rest of Italy ignored the phenomenon and thus started no inquests into their activity, as had been done in the case of Naples and Sicily. As neglected as those regions were, they were still more important than Calabria, which truly ranked at the bottom of the Italian totem pole.

Due to all this neglect, historians lack a clear picture of the early days of the 'Ndrangheta. They know that the organization developed near the capital city of Reggio Calabria, but there is no documentation to explain how and why it came to be a serious force to be reckoned with locally. Only some documentation from early trials suggests a few hints, such as the fact that the organization apparently got its start in the town of Palmi, located where Aspromonte meets the Tyrrhenian Sea. Inhabited by more than 10,000 people, Palmi was a town where olive trees and grape vineyards provided a valuable source of income to the people, and by Calabrian standards, Palmi was relatively large in 1880. It served as the administrative capital for a region that included 130,000 people, and because of this status, it had governmental offices, a courtroom, a police station, and a jail. It was precisely in this jail that the most infamous gangsters of Calabria began to organize, making Palmi the first major mafia stronghold in Calabria.

Aerial views of Palmi

The first sign of mafia activity came in the early months of 1888 when *picciotti* in bars and brothels started engaging in knife battles – with the losers refusing to report to the police who had slashed them. Picciotti were now involved in low level acts of criminality, such as extorting money from prostitutes and gamblers, and threatening landlords with vandalism if they did not pay them protection money – the cornerstone of mafia activity. As these activities ramped up, the *picciotti* engaged in turf warfare and, thus, settled the score with their rivals through these public knife fights. After several months of this, a government clerk got caught in the crossfire of one of these fights, forcing the police to jump into action: the first twenty-four *picciotti* were arrested in 1889, giving historians a snapshot of what kind of person was involved in these activities. The majority of them were in their late teens and early twenties, and they worked in jobs such as agricultural work (peasants, shepherds), as well as hospitality (waiters) and other low wage jobs. Only a few had their own land, and the "boss" was a cobbler who, at the age of sixty, was by far the oldest man in the group. Another common denominator amongst these twenty-four *picciotti* was that every single one of them had already spent time in jail, an experience that shaped their gangster tactics. In fact, historians argue that the 'Ndrangheta was not founded as much as fully formed from within the prison system, a commonality it shares with the Neapolitan Camorra.

Trials persisted throughout the last decade of the century, providing the small scraps of evidence that historians now use to reconstruct the world of the 'Ndrangheta. In the 1892 trial, they learned that the *picciotti* received tattoos that signaled their place in the clan hierarchy. They also had a distinctive uniform, with tight pants that flared over their shoes, wore their silk scarves in a certain way, and even had their own distinct hairstyle: a pompadour shaped like a butterfly. However successful these trials were (especially compared to the paltry success of Sicilian and Neapolitan law enforcement), they were no match for nature: when another earthquake hit Calabria and destroyed Palmi in 1894, law and order could not keep control, and soon the *picciotti* were thriving again, making the most of the chaos that surrounded them.

After another two years, in 1896, law enforcement was able to make another series of arrests and extract more confessions from the *picciotti*. During the trial, the prosecutors were able to learn about the details of the ranks and rituals of the 'Ndrangheta. According to the confessions, the *picciotti* formed themselves into cells or sections, based on geographical location. Cells were all divided hierarchically into a higher and a lower section, known as a Minor Society and a Major Society. The lower ranking men were referred to as the *picciotti* and the higher ranking men were known as the camorristi. Each society had a boss and a bookkeeper (contaiolo in local dialect) who kept track of and redistributed any gang income. In order to join the society at the lowest rank of "Honored Youth," the boss had to convene all his men in a circle within a dark room and perform a ceremony that required every member to signal that he was "comfortable" with the new recruit.

In the earliest evidence about the 'Ndrangheta, it becomes clear that there are countless similarities with the Camorra, from their shared illegal activities (exploiting prostitution and gambling) to their fashion choices, their organizational structure, their preferred punishments of their enemies, and even their founding myth. In fact, this is no coincidence; nor is it a sign that the Calabrian mafia was simply an offshoot of the Neapolitan mafia. Instead, it points to the fact that the two mafias emerged out of the same brutal, poorly organized prison system that was founded during the Neapolitan Bourbon reign.

Another early mafia trial, whose records miraculously survived all the earthquakes, speaks to the first schemes, rituals, and habits of the *picciotti* in the town of Africo around the early 1890s. In that town, the typical musical instrument was known as the zampogna, which is roughly the same as a Scottish bagpipe and made of cured animal skin. In November 1894, there was a bagpipe party taking place on the streets of Africo, with men skipping around the musician, a man named Giuseppe Sagoleo. He eventually confessed his involvement in the mafia to the investigators.

According to his story, Sagoleo was a reluctant recruit to the mafia. He had been invited to join by an ex-prisoner named Domenico Callea, who was considered one of the leaders of what he described as a "secret society." Normally, joining cost seven and a half lire (nearly the price of a goat in those days), but Callea offered to let Sagoleo join for free. Before agreeing, Sagoleo decided to find out more about the society, and it turned out that their main activities were not just drinking wine and having fun, as they claimed. They were also prone to violence, including beating people who refused to join and, worse, committing all sorts of crimes at the leaders' behest. Ultimately, Sagoleo decided to reject Callea's offer, as it seemed like an unhealthy pyramid scheme that profited the bosses with little benefit to the lower ranks. Indeed, this imbalance meant that in the early years, many new recruits were willing to betray the society and confess everything to the police, which is why it took several decades for the organization's development to really take off.

Despite his refusal, Sagoleo could not escape the attention of Callea and his friends, who often forced him to play his zampogna for them or else risk having his instrument destroyed. This kind of bullying (called *prepotenza*) was a key part of the *picciotteria* strategy. They liked to make their presence felt throughout every aspect of society, with the hopes of undermining the community and make its members feel anxiety and fear. Other acts of *prepotenza* included stealing livestock from local peasants and cooking and eating the stolen animals in public. With the help of butchers also in the organization, the *picciotti* were able to steal upwards of 70 pigs in a single year, causing the legal livestock trade to collapse. Thanks to their experience in the mountains of Aspromonte, they also engaged in cattle rustling, stealing all the cows in one place and then transporting them to friends and family elsewhere for safekeeping. The bosses also liked to show off their wealth and power by doing extravagant and difficult things, like treating a large group of guests to a seafood dinner at a time when seafood was virtually impossible to come by.

Also during these early stages, the *picciotti* were able to make important connections with local military tribunals, enlisting local judges by putting them on their payroll. Thanks to the constant neglect of the Italian authorities, who did little more in Calabria than collect taxes and demand military service from the local men, the *picciotti* were able to continue developing their regime with little interference.

This situation changed in 1894, when Sergeant Angelo Labella, a police commander, started to report on the criminal organization he had discovered. Among the fifty members he had uncovered was Domenico Callela. In response to the investigation, the *picciotti* stepped up their efforts at intimidation, slaughtering animals and leaving their carcasses to rot in public. They also vandalized farms and orchards, and they left death threats for possible witnesses. The bagpiper, Sagoleo, was used as part of this campaign of intimidation - they marched him around the town, forcing him to play music as they improvised words to songs that threatened their enemies.

One of the most brutal murders of this time was carried out on an ex-member of the *picciotti* known as Pietro Maviglia. He had betrayed the brother of Domenico Callea and was expelled from the group. Sergeant Labella had planned to use Maviglia as one of his witnesses, so the other members decided it was time to silence him for good. In order to set their plan into motion, Callea and the bosses decided to make peace with Maviglia. On the night of All Saints, they planned a bagpipe party to celebrate his re-entry, and during the party, they led him away with the offer of eating a newly slaughtered goat. When he was found four days later, he was lying on top of his walking stick in a field, 15 minutes away from where the party had been held. He had five lesions on his body, in his skull, and in his heart. His throat was slashed clean across so that undigested food was emerging from his esophagus. Salt was sprinkled on the wound as if the killers wanted to ingrain their sense of vendetta even deeper. Maviglia had been butchered like the animal they had offered to serve him as a gesture of peace.

The Maviglia murder was a brutal signpost planted by the *picciotti* to demonstrate just how remorseless they were. They did not hide the body, which was mutilated beyond the point of necessity to instill fear in all around them. At the same time, such a brutal killing was impossible to ignore on the part of the authorities, so the loss of a potential witness did not deter them from continuing their investigation. A growing military presence amassed in the town of Africo, which allowed more witnesses to start to come forward. Sergeant Labella capitalized on this newfound source of power to extract as much evidence as possible from willing collaborators. Soon, Maviglia's murderers were discovered and arrested, and during the interrogation they turned on one another, breaking the code of silence as they confessed.

Thanks to this breach in secrecy, investigators learned of an important religious element to the *picciotti* secret society, one that continues on to the present day. The members of the society were all part of an important ritual at the Sanctuary of the Madonna of Polsi, a sacred space hidden in a valley of Aspromonte where it is believed that the Virgin Mary appeared to a shepherd in 1144. Every year, a festival brings tens of thousands of locals to a small church, who bring offerings and shout vows before parading around a statue of the Madonna. The chief bosses of the 'Ndrangheta take advantage of the chaos and the sacred nature of the event in order to convene in secrecy. Recently, prosecutors have claimed that the Duisberg massacre of 2007 was planned during this festival, and more than a century prior, in September 1894, a witness claimed to have observed the bosses convening there as well, possibly planning the Maviglia murder.

In the end, Sergeant Labella was able to piece together a narrative about the start of the 'Ndrangheta that historians accept today as roughly accurate. He believed the organization started no later than 1887 with the release of an important member from prison, though this date was disputed by others at the time, suggesting that perhaps it started as early as 1879. The way it got its start was that as Calabrian criminals were released from jail, they started to form a loose association, offering each other help and collaborating on small criminal projects. At first, they lacked the necessary support to go any further than these isolated acts of crime, but in the 1880s, when an economic crisis hit Calabria and decimated its agricultural economy, the isolated Calabrian ex-cons knew the situation was ripe for exploitation. At this time, they were able to find plenty of men and boys willing to join them in their activities, and the poor economic situation coincided with the arrival of the railway in Calabria, bringing an influx of new people and possible jobs that intensified the power of the new bosses. As they were better able to infiltrate certain industries, they could offer their new recruits better paying positions in exchange for loyalty.

Electoral reforms that were taking place in Italy at the time increased the size of the voting electorate and also gave the local government more freedom and more money. Local politics started to become a more remunerative business, and the increase in money brought an increase in violence as candidates and parties would physically threaten and harm one another in the search for votes. This unhealthy environment was one in which the *picciotti* and their toxic attitudes thrived, and the police, unfortunately, preferred to avoid investigating such behaviors in fear of their own safety.

In short, Calabria's ruling class proved utterly unable or unwilling to deal with the steady rise of the deadly criminal organization growing in their midst. This failure is perhaps no surprise, as some of the *picciotti* were actually close family members of illustrious politicians, providing that essential kinship tie between them that has served as the backbone for all of the mafias of Italy. For every success that law enforcement secured against them, and their early success is notably stronger than it was in the case of the other mafias that seemed completely resistant to prosecution, they suffered irreparable setbacks. As the historical record shows in the case of the Maviglia murder, although the criminals were convicted, they served incredibly short sentences, and they served those sentences in the very same jails where they had learned their criminal behavior in the first place, thus reinforcing their ties to the organization rather than loosening them.

The Cuocolo Trial

The new Italian government had gotten off to a rocky start, and indeed the fragile coalition of the Right would not be able to hold on for very long, soon cracking under the pressure of the failing economy. At the end of the 19th century, vast changes began to take place in Italian society, including the rise of the socialists and the workers' strikes that accompanied it. On the one hand, with the introduction of electoral suffrage for all men in 1882 and the development of the economy, the Camorra was able to expand out of the lower classes and reach more confidently into the worlds of business and politics. On the other hand, they were still being scrutinized by northern politicians, a pressure that would eventually force the Camorra into a long period of decline.

The real turning point in the Camorra's history came during the Saredo Inquiry of 1901, a government investigation into the problems of Naples led by Senator Giuseppe Saredo. The inquiry resulted in a report of 2,000 pages and concluded with a damning indictment of Neapolitan society.[138] This inflammatory conclusion did not result in any kind of action, but it did generate widespread anger across the south, as journalists rejected what they deemed another "lecture" from the north and demanded more money. With this increased attention to the city, living standards actually improved, which perhaps contributed more than anything else to the decline of the Camorra. Moreover, this was the period of time when many Neapolitans started to immigrate to America, which transferred much of the criminal activity across the Atlantic. A third reason for the decline of the Camorra can be attributed to the rise of other possible associations, including workers' unions that came along with the rise of socialism.[139] Fourth, the Neapolitan Camorra did not prove as savvy in learning to manipulate the new media environment as their Sicilian counterparts showed themselves to be.

---

[138] Tom Behan, *The Camorra: Political Criminality in Italy* (New York: Routledge, 2005).

[139] Felia Allum, *Camorristi, Politicians and Businessmen: The Transformation of Organized Crime in Post-War Naples* (New York: Routledge, 2017), n. 20.

Saredo

Aside from these broader contextual factors, a major turning point came during the reign of Prime Minister Giovanni Giolitti, a man who had become an expert in co-managing the city of Naples alongside the mob bosses. The event that nearly ended the Camorra was known as the Cuocolo case, and it took out Big 'Enry, the last supreme boss of the Honored Society in Naples.

Giolitti

The Cuocolo case began in 1906 with the discovery of the bloody body of Maria Cutinelli, who had suffered 13 stab wounds. A hunt for her husband, Gennaro Cuocolo, turned up his body not far away, and investigators found he had been stabbed 47 times and had his skull smashed to bits. His body was left out on display, positioned so that the corpse mingled with the refuse that was being pumped out of the local slaughterhouse. The Camorra's involvement in the double homicide was never in doubt, and five men were arrested, including Big 'Enry, but the entire group had been seen in public eating a dinner during the time of the murders, so they were set free.

The case remained at a standstill until the next year, when an internal power struggle within the branches of the Italian police force caused the case to be transferred to a different authority, the Carabinieri (the military police). Thanks to their involvement, they were able to secure a remarkable witness, Gennaro Abbatemaggio,[140] who broke the Camorra's code of *omertà* (the code of secrecy and silence) and testified in court to the entire plan behind the Cuocolo murders, saying that he had witnessed the key planning decisions in person. According to the witness, the Camorra had decided to murder Cuocolo because he had betrayed his partner to the police in an effort to keep all the loot from a burglary for himself. Over the course of the trial, however, Abbatemaggio's credibility fell apart, as he was shown to have planted corroborating evidence, and the case risked collapsing. Then the police force, angered about having been elbowed out of the case, came back with their own accusations, to which Abbatemaggio countered with a new set of accusations of his own.

All these salacious and gruesome details of backstabbing at all levels made for excellent journalism, and the newspapers covered the case with relish. Thanks to the Cuocolo case, it became apparent that the Camorra had reached every corner of society, and details about the gangsters' habits became public. It was discovered that they plotted their crimes in one of the city's most illustrious public spaces, and that the supposedly "proper" upper classes were addicted to gambling and borrowing money from the Camorra to finance their habits. Newspapers started to bid on scoops, competing with one another to secure more extravagant stories as witnesses sold statements to the police and the Carabinieri. In the end, the investigation took nearly five years and cost hundreds of thousands of lire.

---

[140] Umberto Santino, *Mafia and Antimafia: A Brief History* (Bloomsbury Publishing, 2015), 167.

In March 1911, the trial finally took place in the town of Viterbo, north of Rome, five years after the double murder took place. 41 men stood accused of the murder, and Abbatemaggio was a star witness, despite the odd twists and turns his story had taken. Big 'Enry testified, eloquently, in his own defense. A combined 779 witnesses and defendants traded insults and, in some cases, even spat at each other from across the courtroom, and the case made such news that even the *New York Times* reported on it.

In July 1912, the 41 defendants were ready to hear their fate. When the guilty sentence was passed down, one of them slit his own throat with a broken piece of glass in the courtroom. The judge sentenced them to more than 400 years in prison for their crimes relating to murder and membership in a criminal association.

The end result was what the Italian state wanted, but the means to achieve it were questionable at best, earning the nation terrible press overseas for the circus-like atmosphere and suspicious judicial practices. The state proved incapable of answering basic questions, like how to make deals with criminal defectors, lessons that remained unlearned for decades and caused no end of chaos. All of it frustrated future efforts to fight organized crime, but the trial was also remarkable because it effectively ended the Honored Society. After the trial, there were no more reports of any kind of criminal activity, most likely because the police force had been openly discredited in front of the entire Italian public, which robbed the Camorra of its secret partner in crime co-management. In fact, reliable witnesses from the trial suggested that the Camorra was already on the downswing before the sentence had been handed down. The main reason that the Camorra was starting to disintegrate was that it had lost the two foundational principles that had made it seem invincible: the promise of dividing the profits of crime amongst all members, and that of *omertà*. Those two principles kept a strong bond amongst the members, but it was being replaced with a "winner takes all" mentality. Whereas strength had previously been derived from the group's unity, now single charismatic leaders were little better than thugs exerting power over a small group of subservient men. Evidence of this disintegration could be found in the very actions of a man like Gennaro Abbatemaggio: had the code of *omertà* remained strong, he never would have come forth to make his accusations in so brazen a manner.

During the trial, one witness testified that the Camorra was relaxing its standards and considering the admission of men who had already been "dishonored" in reputation. Big 'Enry then stepped in with his testimony to save the honor of the Camorra and restore it to its glorious past, but what historians glean from this almost complete downfall is that the Camorra had not been able to modernize in Naples. Since they came from the lower classes of society, they had been unsuccessful in making a complete leap into the upper reaches. They could sometimes secure the cooperation of politicians, but they were unable to put their own men into office. At best, they could perform important services for the state, but they could not, themselves, infiltrate the state. Thus, as they remained stuck in the position of a criminal elite within the lower classes, the Neapolitan Camorra was unable to withstand the shifts of contemporary political life and could not resist the blows it was dealt from the northern politicians. According to legend, on May 25, 1915, the last free Camorristi met in a bar and dissolved the Honored society.

In a bizarre coda to this incredible case, in 1927, Abbatemaggio, looking for a change of fortune, declared that he had given false testimony in the case. In the wake of that claim, the incarcerated Camorristi who were still alive were granted an early release.

Cosa Nostra Comes to America

The mafia grew quickly due to several lucky breaks it had in terms of its relationship to the fledgling Italian government. Most historians mark 1890 as the moment marking Cosa Nostra's passage from local menace to sophisticated criminal organization, with tentacles reaching into the highest levels of politics and blood on its hands. Thanks to connections at the highest levels of Italian politics, the mafia was able to spread beyond Sicily and Italy's borders across the Atlantic to the United States.[141]

The mafia's emigration from the island of Sicily was also the result of (or at least facilitated by) external forces. Due to the civil unrest and its underlying cause (poor living conditions) in the first decade of the 20th century, nearly 25% of the population of the island emigrated, and of the 1.1 million Sicilians seeking fortunes elsewhere, 800,000 went to the United States. [142] Among them were members of the mafia, some of whom were already on the run from the authorities, while others sought to develop more lucrative opportunities overseas.

Palermo and New York were connected via the lemon trade as early as the 1880s. Beyond New York, Sicilians settled in New Orleans, where the police chief was murdered in 1890, a tragic, dramatic event leading to the lynching of Sicilian suspects.[143] In fact, as early as 1891, new Italian immigrants had already earned themselves a negative reputation - *The New York Times* printed references to "Italian assassins" and "Italian murders," using the term "mafia" to describe their organization.[144]

Among the many discussions surrounding the mafia's arrival in the United States, two were most prevalent. One was developed at the time of the mass Sicilian migration, and one was born in the 1960s and 1970s. In the early days of the mafia in the United States, people hypothesized that its arrival was a concerted effort on Italy's part to dump its criminals, amounting to nothing short of an invasion. It was only later that descendants of Italian immigrants integrated into American society revised this fable, claiming that the Sicilian immigrants were simply peasants who had to adapt their rural traditions to the grim reality of big city life. They claimed the mafia

---

[141] Dickie 2015:15

[142] This was the largest mass migration in European history for reasons other than outright religious persecution or ethnic pogroms (De Stefano, 2007, p. 19).

[143] Dickie 2015:162

[144] Maselli and Candeloro 2004:36

was the result of alchemy between old Sicilian values of family and honor and the dark side of the American dream. Both, of course, were a gross misinterpretation of Sicilian society, which was less antiquated than sophisticated.[145]

The Cosa Nostra established a network making it integral in every step of the immigration process. In order to get a job prior to departure, an immigrant was affiliated with a boss - who used threats to bring a sector of the market under his control, for example, in construction - under the *padrone* system. The immigrant would be further indebted to the boss as the boss advanced him the price of his steamer ticket, only to recoup it with interest. These immigrants lived in cramped quarters, with 8,200 Sicilians residing on a single street in New York City - Elizabeth Street - in 1905. Effectively a tenement, the street was crowded with sweatshops where the immigrants worked.

Americans were both frightened and saddened by this fast-growing neighborhood, their prejudice preventing them from seeing that the area was growing and improving by leaps and bounds. Within this developing neighborhood, the mafia, unfortunately, managed to transplant and defuse itself, using the two trademark skills it had honed at home. First, it was able to use its speed and versatility to leap into new business initiatives, such as cornering the market on the trade of a certain drug. This flexibility came from the way the mafia network was structured, with each boss authorized to take the Cosa Nostra brand in whatever direction he chose, as long as he had the okay of his superiors back home. Second, it relied on the long game. This meant they had to set up a number of important connections to allow their *cosche* to spread outside of western Sicily. This included protection rackets, connections with local politicians, diplomatic relations with other cosche, and the cultivation of a positive public image in which they had to be patient and exacting. Interestingly, the technique paid dividends in the United States, though it was not nearly as effective outside of western Sicily. Even today, after more than a century and a half, the Cosa Nostra only managed to expand in limited ways in the rest of Sicily and the Italian mainland.[146]

The U.S. and Italy were perceived as two different worlds, new and old, coexisting in transatlantic connections the mafia honed in their economic interest. Regardless of any laws, goods, newspapers, communication, and money regularly crossed the ocean, maintaining and strengthening Italian and American ties. These ties proved seriously lucrative when, in the 1920s, the U.S. instituted prohibition. These laws cracked down on alcohol and narcotic use and distribution in an effort to lead citizens back to the "virtues" of the Founding Fathers, aligning them with the principles of Fordism, which argued that every element of a workers' life had to be regulated in the interest of productivity.

Prohibition had the opposite effect instead. The passing of the Eighteenth Amendment caused

---

[145] Dickie 2015:163
[146] Dickie 2015:164

bootlegging industries to spring up, presenting massive opportunities for illegal activity.[147] The primary beneficiaries of this criminality were the Sicilian, Irish, and Jewish immigrants who seized upon this very American way of doing business. Smuggling networks were also developed, accompanied by a rise in violence. Due to ambiguities in the law, bootleggers were able to present themselves as simple businessmen, allowing them to openly entrench themselves in commercial activity. This did nothing to deter them from regularly bribing policemen and politicians, establishing mutually beneficial relationships with lasting effects.

Of the 17 major bootleggers in New York in the 1920s, only three were Italian, but Prohibition enabled them to enter mainstream criminal business, moving the Cosa Nostra beyond the bounds of the tenements of Little Italy.[148] It also allowed Sicilian organized crime to acquire a more broadly Italian dimension as the melting pot of New York City served to bring Italian immigrants together from across the peninsula. It was a particularly good time for mafioso to emigrate out of Italy, as Fascist Benito Mussolini's rise to power led to a massive crackdown on criminal activity and a wholesale disruption of the way of doing business that the mafia had so carefully cultivated. During this time, it was believed that around 500 mafiosi escaped prosecution by emigrating to the United States, where they found a climate ripe for their illegal dealings.

Though Prohibition allowed the mafia to gain a lucrative foothold, it also resulted in the stereotyping of Italian Americans as gangsters. During this period, there were a million Italians in New York City alone, and while only a small proportion of them were criminals, the reputation attached itself to the entire ethnic group.[149]

Prohibition gave the most famous Italian American mobster, Charles "Lucky" Luciano, his start. Born in Sicily in 1897, he left the island in 1905 at the age of 9. Already in trouble with the law for unlawful possession of narcotics at 18, Prohibition helped to turn him into a high-profile criminal gangster. He was famous for the large scars on his neck, which he received when a rival gang kidnapped him, slashed him, and left him for dead in 1929 (his unlikely survival of this incident is what inspired his nickname).

Lucky's story is not only remarkable for the scope of the criminal activity he conducted, from prostitution rings to trafficking, but also the way in which it also points to the way in which the Cosa Nostra intersected with - and benefited from - the formal participation of the U.S. government. After being imprisoned for 30-50 years for his prostitution racket (where he continued to run his crime organization), Lucky's sentence was commuted. It is unclear as to

---

[147] According to one statistic, it is estimated that millions of Americans drank throughout the 1920s (Lupo, 2015, ch. 2). It is believed that Prohibition infused $2 billion into the illegal economy until it was struck down in 1933 (Dickie, 2015, p. 175).

[148] Lupo 2015. Another statistic suggests that while 50 per cent of bootleggers were of Jewish origin, only 25 per cent were Italian.

[149] Dickie 2015:178. See also Reppetto, 2016.

exactly why, but the prevailing story is that the U.S. Navy asked him to go to Sicily to work for their intelligence operations by connecting with local fishermen who might have information about enemy submarine activity, with the understanding that he would be voluntarily deported from the United States. [150] There is no evidence to indicate this deal actually took place, but after only 10 years, Lucky was released and deported to Italy, allowing him to continue on his criminal path until he died of a heart attack in 1962. [151]

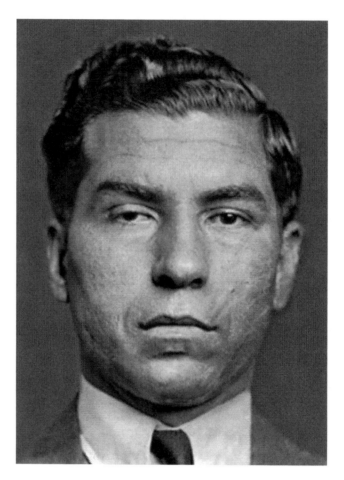

Lucky Luciano

For much of its existence in the United States, the Cosa Nostra appeared to be an inevitable part of life, especially in large cities such as New York City and Chicago. For a long time, the mafia's worst bosses seemed immune to prosecution, as the locals simply chose to turn a blind eye, either because they lacked the resources or the courage to do otherwise, or because they were simply being paid off. The federal government was not much more effective in their efforts. Unbelievably enough, even as late as the 1960s, the FBI still managed to dispute that an American branch of the Cosa Nostra actually existed.[152]

---

[150] Newark 2012:99

[151] Dickie 2015:194. Upon his return to Italy, Luciano decided to settle not in Palermo as might be expected, but in Naples, which he used as a base to organize illegal narcotics trafficking (Dickie, 2015, p. 238).

Once J. Edgar Hoover left the FBI in 1972, the agency started to dedicate serious resources to the control of organized crime, culminating in a massive success in the late 1970s when the federal government endeavored to eliminate the Cosa Nostra once and for all. Although the effort was not a complete success, it was the biggest such action of the 20th century, utilizing electronic surveillance, undercover agents, and plenty of mafia informants. It culminated in the conviction of 23 bosses, including the infamous John Gotti of the Gambino family of New York City.[153]

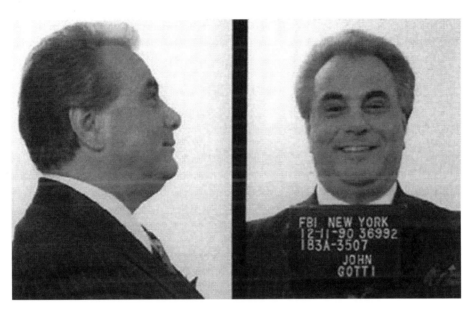

Gotti

Fascism

Much of Italian history is intertwined with the rise and fall of fascism, and the history of the Cosa Nostra – intricately interwoven with the history of the Republic of Italy – is no exception. When Prime Minister Benito Mussolini declared his dictatorship in front of Parliament in January 1925, he made a commitment to crush all forms of resistance, any kind of opposition to his absolute authority, and, by extension, that of his gangs. A consequence of this show of power was that immediately afterwards, the people of Sicily decided to support him, realizing that it was better to have a friend in high places rather than an enemy. Initially, Mussolini personally enjoyed fantastic public popularity in Sicily, but he soon lost it when the people realized that his national government was no different than any other in terms of the poor attention actually paid to the needs of this island region.

---

[152] Jacobs, Panarella, and Worthington, 3.
[153] Jacobs, Panarella, and Worthington, 5.

Mussolini

Soon it became clear how Mussolini would be able to win true support in Sicily: he would make the mafia his enemy in the south, just as he had made socialism his enemy in the north. This made a very convenient narrative, one that would also yield the benefit of allowing Mussolini to sweep away some politicians who had been held over from the pre-fascist, liberal regime, who still attracted a measure of loyalty from the people and, thus, weakened Mussolini's stranglehold on the island. Mussolini's resolve was intensified further when, in 1924, he visited Sicily for the first time and the mayor of a small town, a known mafioso by the name of Don Francesco Cuccia, committed a serious breach of etiquette. He told Mussolini he should do without his personal bodyguards and allow Don Cuccia to take care of his protection. Deeply offended and no doubt unsettled, Mussolini immediate appointed an important law enforcement official to Trapani to start looking into the 216 murders that had been committed in the Marsala region that year alone. This man, Cesare Mori, soon was made prefect of Palermo, and endowed with the full authority to go after the Cosa Nostra, with the hopes of strengthening the power of the regime. Not only did he do that, he planned a major anti-Mafia offensive that would take place the next year.

Within a year after his declaration of dictatorship, Mussolini had instituted a war on organized crime in Sicily that started on January 1, 1926 in the town of Gangi. In the bitter cold of the high mountain elevation, the police made massive arrests and pushed the mafiosi up the slopes to their headquarters. The law enforcement agents cut all forms of communication and blocked the access to the roads below. With the area secured, the police headed up into the mountains themselves, determined to do Mussolini's bidding. Slowly, they managed to make headway, taking just one day to capture the first bandit, an older man named Gateano Ferrarello, who was known as "king" of the mountain. He demanded that he be allowed to surrender himself to the mayor, and then he committed suicide while in jail.

The rest of the operation took much longer to carry out. The fascist police had to resort to all sorts of violent tactics, including confiscating, slaughtering and selling off the people's livestock, and even taking hostages amongst the women and children. According to rumor, in some cases, Mussolini's men even raped the bandits' female family members. 10 days later, the bandits showed no sign of giving up, so that Cesare Mori, now the leader of the fascist police force, stood in front of the people of Gangi and made an impassioned – and rather patronizing – plea to the entire town, encouraging them even while he threatened them that they had to rise up against the bandits and force them to turn themselves in. The speech was a success, and within a few days the fascist police had managed to arrest 130 fugitives and 300 accomplices.

Mori

Beyond the success in actually capturing those wanted men, the siege of Gangi was a spectacular achievement for fascist propaganda, allowing the new dictatorship to prove to the Italian people that they were tough on crime. Effectively, thanks to this new image, the mafia went into hibernation, or at least that was what Mussolini's official records suggested.[154]

After his phenomenal success with the siege of Gangi, Mori continued to prosecute mafiosi, setting his sights on a man named Don Vito Cascio Ferro who had been working between the United States and Sicily, working as a cattle smuggler. This prosecution went even more smoothly, with the help of an interprovincial anti-mafia police force, and Cascio Ferro was arrested, along with more than 150 suspects. Receiving a life sentence at his 1930 trial, Cascio Ferro died behind bars in 1942.[155]

As part of these shows of power, Mori decided to harness the dramatic techniques of the fascist regime. He decided to stage massive public speeches during which he demanded the audience swear their loyalty to fascism: they were forced to sign papers and even were given badges to wear to proclaim their allegiance on their clothing. Rather than rely on justice, Mori decided to operate with brute force, to great success. He simply pressured the wealthy landowners to give up the criminals they had been working with, and within three years he had arrested more than ten thousand people. Historians can confidently assert, however, that by no means were all of these men part of the Honored Society. Many were not even actually members of minor bandit networks. In fact, there is no question that innocent people were swept up alongside the criminals in these fascist dragnets, which creates yet another gray area in the history of the mafia as it intersects with fascism. As helpful as these round-ups were, they were also highly problematic. Aside from the completely innocent, Mori was also responsible for many miscarriages of justice, including the aggressive prosecution of a man who was accused of stealing a single donkey. While this man could have been a boss, an unlucky client, or just a regular citizen, he was found dead in his jail cell awaiting trial, likely due to foul play.

Despite this aggressive, apparently successful prosecution, fascism by no means extinguished the Cosa Nostra, as many of the organization's most ambitious figures moved to the United States. Amongst those who stayed, some learned that bribery was still an effective tool under fascism. A boss of central Sicily, Giuseppe Genco Russo, was able to be repeatedly acquitted of countless charges against him, no doubt because of his ability to bribe the right people.

Cesare Mori ended his tenure as prefect of Palermo in 1929 after more than three and a half years on the job because, according to the regime, his task was completed: the mafia had been permanently dismantled. In reality, he had been removed by Mussolini because he had fallen out of favor, and upon his return from Sicily he was given a minor post from which he could attract little public notice. His successor continued prosecuting the mafia, however, as it was by no

---

[154] Dickie, *Cosa Nostra,* 145-147.
[155] Dickie, *Cosa Nostra,* 154-5.

means all taken care of. Instead, he avoided round-ups or show trials and simply sent suspects into internal exile without due process, a common method used by the regime for dealing with any manner of enemies.

For the next decade, the mafia stayed largely underground until Mussolini fell in 1943 and the mafia was resuscitated by the United States.[156]

World War II and the Rebirth of the Cosa Nostra

The Allies' invasion of Italy during World War II represented another turning point in history, whether or not it can be fully credited with bringing Sicilian-American gangsters back to the island's shores. What Operation Husky did bring for certain was 160,000 troops to Sicily's southeastern coast on July 10, 1943, followed by another 300,000 men who spread across the island.[157] According to one story, an American fighter plane did an odd thing four days later when it flew over the tiny central town of Villalba and dropped a small package. It returned the next day with another package, bearing the words "Uncle Calò," the name of the local mafia boss. Inside was a golden-yellow silk handkerchief, marked with a large letter L. It was a sign from the Allies who soon arrived in town with tanks also painted yellow and depicting an L. Calò went off with them to help them complete the invasion of central Italy. According to the story, Lucky Luciano had been selected for the mission, and the gangster was actually inside one of the tanks. Today, most historians dismiss the story of Don Calò and Lucky Luciano, but locals in Villalba still maintain the veracity of the tale.

Regardless of the actual details, what these lingering uncertainties suggest is that the history of the mafia during and after World War II is still not completely known. Certainly, the powerful role assigned to the U.S. government in this story suggests a desire to shift the blame for the mafia's postwar resurgence to a foreign power. Most likely, the blame deserves to be spread more evenly to a range of different political players.

From this perspective, the story of Uncle Calò is as follows. In 1943, Don Calò led the townspeople to meet the Allied patrol, earning himself the role of mayor after ingratiating himself with the Allies.[158] This account is more in concert with what is known to have happened in Sicily during the Allied invasion, during which the locals welcomed their invaders with open arms, believing they would improve the poor living conditions. Sicilian goodwill toward America no doubt helped increase the joyousness of their welcome. As the fascist leaders were pushed out, the men of honor (who had been exiled) rushed to fill the void, conveniently (and not completely untruthfully) positing themselves as victims of fascism. One high-profile Italian-American mafioso, Vito Genovese, served as the interpreter for American Governor of Sicily Colonel Charles Poletti for the entire six-month occupation.[159] Thanks to his new position of

---

[156] Dickie, *Blood Brothers,* 158-9.
[157] On Operation Husky and its connections to the rise of the mafia, see Newark, 2012, ch. 11.
[158] Heartfield 2012:310

power, Don Calò was able to purge all court and police archives, wiping away all record of his previous criminal activity.[160]

Once the Allies managed to secure Sicily by the middle of August 1943, they set about figuring out how to administer it. They put in place the Allied Military Government of Occupied Territory, or AMGOT, which relied on weak secret service information in its efforts to establish control. One area the British War Office explored was the possibility of using "antifascist" mafia informants to secure the island - the sloppy designation was a clear sign that the British intelligence service did not understand Italian or Sicilian politics. The strategy AMGOT adopted in its clunky attempts to govern was to outlaw all political activity in Sicily during their six-month rule. While it was obvious they had to expunge the fascists, they decided that, as they installed an interim government, they also had to avoid resorting to Left-wing politicians due to their association with communism. Turning to the bosses thus became the logical solution, made possible by the naiveté of AMGOT officials. The bosses seemed the perfect weapon against a possible Communist uprising, as they were clearly unafraid to resort to violence against them as Don Calò had in September 1944, when communists came to give a speech in his town.[161]

By the time Sicily engaged in local politics, the bosses - such as Don Calò - were so cozy with the Allied officials that it appeared Sicily would gain some form of autonomy from Italy by becoming an American protectorate and a mafia-controlled territory.[162]

Meanwhile, the mafia made life miserable for everyday Sicilians as it spread from the cities to rural areas, such as Don Calò's central Villalba. However, the mafioso were openly defiant of - and in some cases, violent toward - Allied soldiers, quickly weakening the Americans' standing in the mind of the locals. [163] As Sicilian gratitude for the liberation was washed away, a rift opened up between Allied occupiers and the Sicilian people, which the mafia - along with the Sicilian Separatist party - was able to exploit for their further gain. By this time, the Allies were ready to support the restoration of a strong Italian state if it meant ending the chaos the mafia blatantly supported.[164]

The Allies may have wanted to end the chaos backed by the mafia, but they wanted to end the chaos even more. Thus, some complex political realignments in Italian politics clarified their newfound, putative anti-mafia stance. In 1946, the mafia severed ties with the Sicilian Separatist movement when they lost votes in the election. From there, they affiliated themselves with the conservative political force, the Christian Democrats.[165] This party was, by no means, a strawman for the mafia. Instead, it was a party standing for family values, which held the

[159] Stille 1996:18
[160] Dickie 2015:196
[161] See Newark, 2012, p. 240.
[162] Dickie 2015:199
[163] Williams 2018:38
[164] Newark 2012:291
[165] Newark 2012:292

Vatican's resounding support. The reason the Christian Democrats worked so well with the mafia was due to the party's penchant for favor-based politics, allowing the various Sicilian bosses to create local factions depending on political patronage. It was the way business was carried out in the post-Unification liberal state before fascism disrupted it. In many ways, the rise of the Christian Democrats allowed the situation in Sicily to revert to the status quo.[166]

This affiliation benefited the mafia beyond a simple exchange of favors. Since the relationship was by no means a secret, it gave the mafioso a certain institutional respectability. Moreover, a key part in the United States' strategy to prevent the rise of communism in Italy was keeping the Christian Democrats, and thus the mafia, intact. When the OSS became the CIA in 1947, they maintained that the mafia would effectively enforce the power of the Christian Democrats, and their violent means seemed a fair enough end if it meant stopping the threat of communism. Thanks to the mafia, the Christian Democrats won the election in Sicily in 1948, much to the United States' relief. As a result, regardless of whether there was an active Allied plot to restore the mafia to power during the war, they ended up aligning their interests and got reciprocal support.[167]

A major benefit to the relationship between the Christian Democrats and the mafioso was that by 1950, the government had finally addressed the decades-long issue of redistribution of land, with the mafia earning huge dividends from the sales. Moreover, they started to invest in the southern Italian economy, taking the power from local landowners and handing it to the politicians who would determine how government funds were spent. Another benefit to this relationship for both sides was the rate at which Socialists and Communists were murdered in Sicily around election time, including the massacre of Communist farmers in 1947. As the mafia was enlisted as the shadow military arm of this major political force, it was able to murder with impunity; Salvatore Giuliano and his followers - who had carried out the 1947 massacre - bragged about their contribution and even gave newspaper interviews about it.[168]

The 1950s was the era in which the Sicilian Mafia started calling itself "Cosa Nostra." The term is believed to be an American import because Sicilian gangsters wanted to indicate that membership in their group was limited to Sicilians since it was "their thing." Other names for the mafia have been the Brotherhood and the honored society, a name it shares with the Calabrian mafia, the 'ndrangheta.

A lot of what is known about the Cosa Nostra in the early post-war period comes from a man named Tommaso Buscetta, a mafioso who became an informant providing information on the mafia's infiltration of the concrete industry. Buscetta was a snappily dressed womanizer (he claimed to have lost his virginity with a prostitute at the age of 8 for the price of a bottle of olive

---

[166] Dickie 2015:203
[167] Newark 2012:292
[168] Stille 1996:19

oil). His early criminal activity included black market dealings in the war and stealing from the German Army, which allowed him to build up a network in his native city of Palermo. After the liberation, Buscetta went to Naples to fight the Nazis and returned to Palermo a war hero. Buscetta was invited into the Cosa Nostra in 1945 by a small, select family known as the Porta Nuova family. His affiliation with the Cosa Nostra led him to travel in South America and return to Palermo as the city began its concrete transformation.

Buscetta

This transformation, known as the "Sack of Palermo," took place in the 1950s and 1960s. Always mistrustful, Sicilians claimed such actions were directed from Rome. While this is an overstatement, the crazed building boom was the result of the close ties between the Sicilian Mafia and the Christian Democrats. The pattern of postwar rebuilding occurring throughout the country as a part of the economic "miracle" the country experienced was particularly aggressive in Palermo. The hasty zoning laws allowed the destruction of much of its rich architectural legacy, as well as many of its celebrated lemon groves.[169] Now, mafioso kept watch on building sites erected on the land on which lemon groves once stood. A new generation of criminals was building atop the old generation, but they were still using much the same strategy. Enjoying the support of big business and the political establishment (which, in turn, enjoyed the support of the Church), the Cosa Nostra seemed unstoppable.[170] The population of the city doubled in those years, but the center virtually emptied as a result of the careless "building" taking place.[171]

---

[169] Stille 1996:21
[170] Dickie 2015:221-225

The Camorra's Resurrection

Even as the Honored Society was technically dissolved, parts of it remained operational in certain areas of the city, such as the wholesale markets and the docks. Now, instead of the fancy bosses, there were *guappi*, basically street corner bosses who were either former Camorristi of a low level or their sons. These men lacked a stable organization and simply tried to build up their own reputation within the lower class neighborhoods through small-scale trafficking, while aspiring (and usually failing) to gain social mobility.[172]

Moreover, following the dismantling of the Camorra, something important survived: the myth of the heroic Camorrista. Once tales of bloodshed were no longer crowding the newspapers, there was ample room for the romantic stereotype to flourish. Whereas the Camorra had been aggressively misogynistic in every possible way, from their prostitution rackets to the way they violently disciplined their wives and sisters, they were remembered as men of honor who would protect any girl who needed help with a rogue boyfriend or disrespectful husband.

While the city of Naples was no longer the criminal center that it had once been, the surrounding countryside was developing its own set of rules and practices that resembled the early days of the Cosa Nostra in Sicily. Effectively, the Campania countryside was the source of food for the city of Naples. Among the other markets that the Camorra cornered, including produce and cured meats, these countryside mafiosi had an inextricable hold on the Buffalo mozzarella cheese market, an exquisitely creamy delicacy that was highly sought. In the countryside, the mafia set up protection rackets, threatening farmers with violence and destruction if they failed to pay, and in conjunction with that, they infiltrated local government and the judicial system, thus being able to operate with impunity. Until the rise of Mussolini, these criminals stayed out of the limelight, and the only real consequences of their actions were the high food prices that the Neapolitans had to pay.

In the mid-1920s, as Mussolini was consolidating his hold on the Italian government, he decided to target the corruption in the Neapolitan countryside. Mussolini sent Vincenzo Anceschi, a Carabinieri, to lead his powerful anti-Camorra initiative in Campania, and in just two years, Anceschi made 9,143 arrests. In one dramatic event, a funeral was organized for the mysterious death of Vincenzo Serra, the most famous Camorrista figure in the countryside. When the guests were gathered, before the ceremony began, the mourners - presumed mobsters - were rounded up and taken off to prison. This was not a rare, singular occurrence either, because raids at Camorra bosses' funerals became one of Anceschi's signature moves. Although there is scant archival evidence regarding Anceschi's actual trials, it does appear that the campaign in the 1920s was successful, and the Neapolitan countryside was mostly purged of the Honored Society by Mussolini. However, Mussolini made a fatal mistake when he declared the matter of the

---

[171] Stille 1996:22. On the efforts to repopulate the ongoing at the end of the century, see Schneider and Schneider, 2003.

[172] Brancaccio, "Violent Contexts and Camorra Clans," 138.

mafia fully resolved and banned the media from further discussing the question. This diverted public interest from the topic, which inevitably created the ideal conditions for the criminal organizations to reconstitute themselves.

Mussolini

Such was the force of Mussolini's edict that in 1930, Italy's main national encyclopedia pronounced the Camorra dead, describing it as a thing of the past, with only the word itself remaining. Perhaps the only surviving outpost of the Camorra in Naples during the late years of the fascist regime was in a small puppet theater known as the San Carlino, where the audience was treated to old fashioned spectacles with a slightly more recent theme: the battle of the noble Camorristi against corrupt law enforcement. Thus, in fascist and early post-war Naples, "Camorra" appeared to be just a throwback term.

The stereotypes about the Camorra and about the Neapolitan people were more than just nostalgia, however. In fact, they played a significant role in allowing the eventual resurrection and refashioning of the Camorra in the post-war period, and immediately after World War II, Italian politicians wrestling for control fought hard to win over Naples, a city that had voted overwhelmingly against the Republic in the 1946 referendum and remained loyal to the exiled monarchy.

While the whole world was anxious to forget about Naples' sordid past and enjoy the beauty it had to offer, the city itself was equally willing to go along with the act. Newspaper columnists depicted the petty crime of the city with good-natured humor and admiration, even praising the skills of the criminals, who had made their start by dealing in contraband military supplies during the extended wartime Allied occupation of Naples.[173] All the while, these men, known as *correntisti*, were becoming increasingly violent in their tactics. Some publications started referring to these men as *Camorristi*, but soon the usage died out and they were referred to simply as criminals.

Throughout the history of the Camorra, the power of the organization had been closely linked to the power of the nation, and this was certainly the case in the post-war period when, in the late 1950s and early 1960s, Italy experienced an economic "miracle" that exceeded the levels of growth found anywhere else in Western Europe. This "boom" transformed the lives of Italians, who were finally able to get all the modern commodities they desired. Furthermore, it made the Italian lifestyle seem glamorous and fashionable, synonymous with the "sweet life" made famous by Federico Fellini's 1950s film.

As Italy got rich, so too did its most prominent mafias. So skilled were their members in knowing how to reap the benefits of the "boom" that they managed to continue to grow their wealth and power long after Italy's economic growth had slowed in the 1970s.

The first signs of the reemergence of the Camorra in the 1950s came in the form of small and isolated groups of men who extorted, smuggled, and served as unethical middlemen in agricultural markets. As these businessmen quickly accumulated wealth, their violent methods intensified accordingly, but it was unclear at the time which of these men were part of the Camorra and which were simply smugglers and traffickers of a generic sort.[174] This kind of blended criminality is still the case today, as the city's underworld is blurrily divided into various segments, with a Camorra elite at the top of the hierarchy receiving a percentage of the profits in their various territories and then minor criminal groups that have a degree of independence and whose members occasionally transition into the Camorra proper.[175]

By means of their infiltration into the construction industry, their network of tobacco smuggling and narcotics trafficking, as well as their habit of kidnapping and ransoming wealthy victims (including children), the Camorra resurrected itself to the point that the individual *correntisti* and *guappi* coalesced once again into a more organized network. During the 1970s and 1980s, there were 71 kidnappings of victims who were never recovered, even though the families paid the ransoms in at least half those cases.[176] During this period of time, the cigarette-

---

[173] For a fictionalized, first-person account of mafia activities in Allied occupied Naples, and the role that the allies played in helping rehabilitate Neapolitan criminal networks, see the acclaimed text by Norman Lewis, *Naples '44: A World War II Diary of Occupied Italy* (Boston, MA: Da Capo Press, 2004).

[174] Brancaccio, "Violent Contexts and Camorra Clans," 139.

[175] Brancaccio, "Violent Contexts and Camorra Clans," 145.

smuggling market had its own major boom, and most of the key power players in the Camorra today had their start during this period.[177] A major characteristic of the Camorra during the post-war period is that it avoided activities surrounding protection rackets and instead concentrated almost exclusively on illegal commerce.[178]

During this postwar period of prosperity, one of the most famous clans was ruled by Raffaele Cutolo.[179] Don Cutolo was a charismatic leader who imposed a more rigid hierarchy and enjoyed more organizational support than previous bosses, going back to the glory days of Big 'Enry. At the height of his power in the 1970s and early 1980s, Don Cutolo governed approximately 7,000 members, and he was famous for his successful efforts in creating an entire ideology surrounding participation in his mafia. He was able to make his followers feel like they were part of a movement of social and political resistance and thus create a more unified formation than other bosses. In the same vein, he was a savvy communicator who knew how to manipulate the media to communicate covertly with his followers. He also enjoyed grand symbolic gestures that distinguished him from other bosses, both past and future. Most remarkably, he bought a castle on the slopes of Mount Vesuvius, and from this castle he conducted some of his activities in broad daylight, although it did lead to many of his members getting arrested. He himself was sentenced to multiple life sentences in prison in 1995, which did not stop him from getting married and fathering a child while behind bars.[180]

[176] Dickie, *Blood Brotherhood,* 420.
[177] Brancaccio, "Violent Contexts and Camorra Clans," 144.
[178] Brancaccio, "Violent Contexts and Camorra Clans," 149 - 150.
[179] Giuseppe Marrazzo, *Il camorrista. Vita segreta di don Raffaele Cutolo* (Tullio Pironti, 2005).
[180] Brancaccio, "Violent Contexts and Camorra Clans," 140.

A picture of Don Cutolo and his wife

The Rise of the 'Ndrangheta

The rapid ascent of the 'Ndrangheta began in the early 1950s, when the organization began to dominate the area of tobacco trafficking. This practice started during the Allies' occupation of Italy, a phase that lasted even longer in the devastated south as a result of the amphibious operations around Sicily. Cigarettes were covertly transported via the port of Naples, and men who were affiliated with the Allies were able to get special access to this illegal, lucrative activity. Although these traffickers likely did not start out as mafiosi, over time, they began to be affiliated with them.

After the occupation, the second element that gave the 'Ndrangheta new life was the construction of the *Autostrada del Sole* ("The Highway of the Sun"), which connected Salerno (a city south of Naples) to Reggio Calabria. Now Calabria was better connected with the rest of Italy for the first time in its history, which had positive and negative sides. In terms of the development of the 'Ndrangheta, the massive construction project offered opportunities for the *capobastone* to extort money from the northern firms hired to build the highway. They demanded a *pizzo* (protection money, roughly translated as a "squeeze") to keep the construction sites safe, and they inserted themselves into deals for the purchasing and transportation of building materials. As they began their new working relationship, the "gray area" of the

'Ndrangheta started to take shape as mafiosi and legal businessmen made verbal pacts with one another, committing to avoid violence while essentially conspiring to break the law. Thus, the 'Ndrangheta started to enrich itself monetarily and gain a certain veneer of respectability as the public began to see the mafiosi doing business with more illustrious members of society.[181]

Another major shift in the 'Ndrangheta's fortunes came in the 1950s and 1960s as the economic miracle started shifting internal Italian migration patterns, with large numbers of southern Italians moving north to Piedmont and the Veneto as regions became more easily accessible by railway. It is believed that in these decades, over a million Calabrians migrated to the center and north of Italy, and while only a fraction of these migrants were criminals, all Calabrian migrants suffered a certain stigma of guilt by association.[182] In the same vein, major construction projects started in response to a boom in the tourism industry, which offered needed opportunities for work and also allowed the 'Ndrangheta a point of entry into cities such as Turin. Increases in the local murder rates and arson attacks on building sites spiked during these years.

From the construction industry, the 'Ndrangheta was able to spread out and infiltrate local politics. They started murdering their political enemies, racking up a body count of 24 victims in just one small province in the years between 1970 and 1983.[183]

Once again, the state was complicit in the mafia's spread to central and northern Italy because of a new policy that had been instituted in the mid-1950s. Using forced removals, convicted mafiosi were sent to the central and northern regions of Italy, in the hopes that the relocation would serve to sever their ties with their criminal support networks at home. However, this ended up backfiring, as the jailed mafiosi simply relocated their families with them and managed to integrate themselves into their new society upon their release, subsequently serving as a key point of reference for the clan members back home.

The 'Ndrangheta was originally a rural mafia whose business was linked to the money it derived from extortion, kidnapping, and smuggling, and one of the most dramatic and high-profile kidnappings involved a 7-year-old boy in Turin in 1987. He remained in captivity for a year and a half, and in the process he was brainwashed against his parents.[184] The mafia's involvement in kidnapping continued on into the 1990s, and another notorious episode involved holding an 18-year-old boy in underground caves for two years while the 'Ndrangheta negotiated with his family.[185]

The 'Ndrangheta did not make its real mark on the criminal world through these relatively

---

[181] Ciconte, "Origins and Development of the 'Ndrangheta."
[182] Sergi and Lavorgna, 'Ndrangheta, 35.
[183] Varese, Chapter 3.
[184] Dickie, 420.
[185] Antonelli and Nuzzi, *Blood Ties*.

circumscribed criminal acts, but kidnappings did serve a dual purpose. Most importantly, kidnappings earned substantial ransom payments from families and in some cases the state, and such acts struck fear in the hearts of the public, establishing the sense that the mafia could reach anyone. Thus, while this kidnapping and extortion business was developing, the 'Ndrangheta was able to undergo a transformational process and shift from a rural mafia into an entrepreneurial and financial mafia with significant ties abroad.[186] The move abroad was particularly important in the 1980s because Italian law now enabled the government to seize mafia property and funds if their owners were unable to prove that they had been obtained legally. As a result, investing abroad, particularly in Germany, provided an important workaround for the Calabrian mafia[187]

In the 1980s, the discourse concerning the Italian south had started to shift. Once again, politicians believed that the imbalances between northern and southern Italy would get resolved through the increasing modernization taking place. However, the 'Ndrangheta continued to exploit and exacerbate those dynamics, corrupting the modernizing processes so that they would perpetuate the organization's illicit activities. At the same time, the Calabrian mafia perfected the creation of double markets, a process in which an illegal market coexisted with a legal one in a parasitic relationship. They managed to infiltrate and corrupt healthy companies, take them over, and promote their members to high positions.[188]

The mafia was also experimenting with cutting edge technology, unbeknownst to law enforcement. For instance, their drug dealers were the first to use mobile phones capable of scrambling a signal and becoming undetectable, all while the police who were chasing them were still stuck using phone booths. This technological prowess did not just help them avoid detection – cells were able to sell anti-wire-tapping devices to the others, creating another revenue stream.[189]

While the mafia was extending its own reach, the 'Ndrangheta had a stroke of good luck at the expense of the Cosa Nostra. In the early 1990s, the Sicilian mafia carried out two high-profile murders of the anti-mafia judges Giovanni Falcone and Paolo Borsellino. Thanks to these assassinations, the eyes of Italian law enforcement turned with laser-sharp focus to the Cosa Nostra, and with law enforcement preoccupied, the 'Ndrangheta was poised to expand abroad.[190]

---

[186] Renate Siebert, "Mafia Women: The Affirmation of a Female Pseudo-Subject. The Case of the 'Ndrangheta," in *Women and the Mafia*, ed. Giovanni Fiandaca, STUDIES IN ORGANIZED CRIME (New York, NY: Springer New York, 2007), 25, https://doi.org/10.1007/978-0-387-36542-8_3.

[187] Petra Reski, *The Honored Society: A Portrait of Italy's Most Powerful Mafia* (PublicAffairs, 2013), 43.

[188] Ciconte, 42-43.

[189] Antonelli and Nuzzi, *Blood Ties*.

[190] Serenata, "Introduction."

Borsellino

Luigi Oldani's portrait of Falcone

In light of this good fortune, the Calabrians looked to develop their presence in the northern, industrial city of Milan, choosing to make it a central base from which to conduct their shady business transactions. The 'Ndrangheta had already been working in Milan as early as the 1970s by dominating the drug trade there and conducting kidnappings. In that decade, there were more than 150 kidnappings in Lombardy alone.[191] But in the 1990s, these activities gave way to the more sophisticated financial crimes that made Milan an ideal location because of its proximity to Central European countries like Austria and Switzerland, where money could be more easily laundered. As the 'Ndrangheta made itself comfortable, its members started buying local businesses, from bars and pizzerias to gas stations and gyms. They not only formed real estate companies and invested in legal endeavors, but they also created dummy corporations to hide many of their dealings. Before he was murdered, Giovanni Falcone sounded the alarm that the mafia was spreading to the north, and an Anti-Mafia Parliamentary Commission in 1990 was already aware of the presence of Calabrian families in the North and their growing power. The fact that the report was ignored simply marks one more failure on the part of the Italian state.[192]

---

[191] Sergi and Lavorgna, *'Ndrangheta*, 34.
[192] Ciconte, 43-5.

That said, the state did receive some help in the 1990s thanks to a major witness, Filippo Barecca, who received 1.6 billion lire from the government to change his identity and reintegrate into society under a new name. As a mobster, Barecca was involved in the Calabrian narcotics trade, selling 600 kilograms of cocaine per month without being detected by the police at one point. Now, Barecca was one of very few *pentiti* who betrayed the Calabrian mafia, and only he and one other, Franco Pino, were considered important. Barecca came from one of the upper echelons of the "Major Society," having obtained the rank of *santa*, which entitled him to have a dual affiliation with the Freemasons and the mob. It was a highly influential position that also granted him the power to determine the fates of his subordinates. In addition to testifying in trials, Barecca also spoke with journalists ultimately provided the greatest source of inside information on the modern 'Ndrangheta.[193]

The Mafia Wars

On June 30, 1963, a car bomb exploded on a man's property in the small town of Ciaculli, killing a police officer and six other people and burning up thousands of square feet of surrounding tangerine groves. People in Sicily were familiar with car bombs as a part of bloody mafia skirmishes, and some newspapers even claimed they were a good thing, a sign the mafia would eventually eliminate itself. However, the human cost of the Ciaculli car bombing, specifically the seven innocent civilian victims, forced the question of internal mafia violence to the foreground. 100,000 people attended the funeral of the seven victims, bringing with them serious political pressure to take care of the mafia problem. For historians, the Ciaculli car bombing marks the point of no return for the relationship between the mafia and Italian society, forcing the public and the government to reflect on the long history every generation seemed to conveniently forget.[194]

---

[193] Antonelli and Nuzzi, *Blood Ties*.
[194] Dickie 2015:218-219

Pietro Torretto, the mafia boss believed to be responsible for the bombing

While the Ciaculli bomb had been a byproduct of war within the mafia, it also served to set off a war against the mafia.[195] As a result of the Ciaculli car bombing, a crackdown took place across the globe, with 1,903 mobsters being arrested over a few months,[196] but this did not provide concrete answers as to who was responsible.

What is known is that the First Mafia War was the result of a transatlantic drug deal gone bad, leading to a series of car bombings sent by members of rival families to each other, as well as several shootings, one of which took place in the northern city of Milan.[197] It is no surprise that the lack of answers surrounding this case also led to a lack of convictions, and in 1969, the first war against the mafia ended with a series of not-guilty verdicts, putting all the major mafia bosses (including the infamous Totò Riina[198]) back on the streets. They were ready to celebrate their victory, which led to the Second Mafia War.[199]

---

[195] Stille 1996:103.
[196] Stille 1996:103.
[197] Dickie 2015:243.
[198] Bolzoni and D'Avanzo 2015
[199] Stille 1996:104

The years of the Second Mafia War coincide with the post-1968 transformation in Italy, Europe, and the United States. In Italy, the violence was particularly acute and widespread as the extreme Left and Right both engaged in public acts of terrorism, using so many bullets as to earn the 1970s the title the "years of lead."[200] Now, evidence suggests the mafia was involved in helping the extreme Right stage its attacks, including a bomb on the train tracks killing 16 people just before Christmas in 1984.

At the same time that they were engaging in state violence, they were also involved in warfare amongst themselves. Known as the *mattanza* (the slaughter), the final years of the conflict turned Palermo's streets into a war zone, leading to the deaths of around 1,000 people, including mobsters, law enforcement, and innocent bystanders.[201] The major players in the war were the Corleonesi, who gathered support from other families to successfully attack their rivals, the Bontades, the Inzerillos, and the Badalamentis.

After having won the war so decisively, the Corleonesi - headed by Salvatore Riino - assassinated state figures, starting with Colonel Giuseppe Russo in 1977, one of the "eminent corpses" the city had to mourn.[202] As this strategy continued - climaxing in the murders of anti-mafia prosecutors Giovanni Falcone and Paolo Borsellino - more and more *pentiti* (repentant mafioso) came forward to take a stand against the Cosa Nostra.

In 1992, the Cosa Nostra appeared to be flexing its muscles more prominently than ever before when it carried out two of the highest-profile assassinations in Italy after the fall of fascism. On May 23, 1992, Judge Giovanni Falcone, who had been responsible for high-profile mafia convictions, was killed while driving on a Palermo highway along with his wife and three bodyguards after the mafia detonated a bomb containing 400 kilograms of explosives.[203] Two months later, on July 19, Falcone's close friend, prosecutor Paolo Borsellino, and five bodyguards were blown up when Borsellino visited his mother in downtown Palermo.[204] Borsellino had been a neo-fascist in his youth, a fact that elicited scandal, but it was a sign of his anti-mafia stance from a young age because in Sicily, only the fascist regime was willing to make an effort to combat the mafia.[205]

Although Palermo had lost many courageous citizens to the Cosa Nostra, the assassinations in 1992 - in the midst of an election season - represented a particularly ominous moment. In its early history, the Cosa Nostra had only killed two major public figures, Emanuele Notarbartolo (the former mayor of Palermo) in 1893, and Joe Petrosino, a New York police officer shot in 1909. However, since the 1970s and the disappearance of an anti-mafia reporter, that approach

---

[200] Montanelli and Cervi 2013
[201] Pickering-Iazzi 2015:154
[202] Stille 1996:107-108
[203] Dickie 2015:14. For more on Falcone, see Follain, 2012.
[204] Stille 1996:5.
[205] Stille, 1996, p. 25.

changed, culminating in these high profile, spectacular assassinations.[206] Over the course of the next decade, there were several other disappearances and suspicious deaths, and in the late 1970s, it became clear that the mafia was operating according to a new playbook. In one year they killed a journalist, a politician, a policeman, and a judge, and in 1980, there were three more. (The term for this kind of high-profile mafia assassination is "eminent corpse.") There was no mistaking the message of the mafia: as long as the state continued to interfere in its business, no one would be safe. For this reason, these high-profile murders were all carried out in public, and in violent and dramatic ways, in flagrant disregard of the law.

By 1981, a period began that has been referred to as the *mattanza*, a period of daily bloody killings with bodies being disposed of outside police stations or burned in the streets. In response, the Italian government sent General Carlo Alberto Dalla Chiesa to serve as the prefect of Palermo, thanks to his strong track record of fighting the mafia. He was considered a national hero thanks to his success in fighting left-wing terrorism during the "lead years" of the 1970s. Within a few months he, his wife, and their bodyguard were shot to death.

Chiesa

This easy victory gave the Cosa Nostra a sense of invincibility and the belief it had the power

---

[206] Dickie 205: 296.

to do whatever they pleased. The government responded to the mounting number of eminent corpses by passing new anti-mafia legislation that worked to make it a crime to belong to any such criminal organization. It was a similar law to the anti-Racketeer RICO law passed in the United Sates in 1970, and this new law, along with a provision that allowed the state to confiscate the illegal earnings of the mafia, would have given the state a powerful new tool when used properly. However, the state never did try to use them to their fullest extent, as the list of eminent corpses just got longer. While people had long compared the city to New York City and Chicago, with the number of car bombs and shootings occurring in Palermo, the Sicilian capital seemed more like war torn Beirut.

The mid-1980s brought a turning point as Tommaso Buscetta had agreed to collaborate with law enforcement, leading to over 300 arrest warrants being issued. This did not mean it was smooth sailing, as the murders kept on taking place and the police officers threatened mass mutiny in response to their very obvious lack of safety, but Italy was able to grind its way towards what was known as a maxi trial, one that would be prosecuted by Giovanni Falcone and Paolo Borsellino.

Falcone and Borsellino were old friends by the time they set out to prosecute the historic maxi trial. Born at around the same time, they grew up in the same neighborhood of Palermo, one to a chemist and the other to a pharmacist. Despite their very different political convictions (Falcone was leftist while Borsellino was briefly a neo-Fascist), the two shared a number of important values, such as their devotion to their country and their belief in the power of justice. Falcone was a pessimist who suffered in his daily commute to work, which required a convoy of four bulletproof cars and machine-gun toting agents, followed by a helicopter. Borsellino tended to see the bright side of things.

The trial began in 1986 and lasted for two years. It took place in a massive bunker next to the prison and was built especially for the trial. The 200 most dangerous defendants were placed in cages, while at least 119 were still on the run. Palermo was tense and quiet, as the remaining mafiosi had decided to lay low during the trial and not commit any more acts of violence.

The citizens of Palermo were divided in their feelings about the trial. One prominent Sicilian writer, Leonardo Sciascia, was against the trial, despite his outspoken opposition to the mafia. He believed that the trial itself was being conducted in an unjust manner and threatened to rely on the similarly unethical tactics of fascism. More than just a lone voice of an aging intellectual, Sciascia's misgivings spoke to the fact that Sicilians were, as a people, deeply mistrustful of the Italian state, the consequences of which were dire.

The maxi trial finally was able to deliver a collective verdict in December 1987, with 114 of the 474 defendants being acquitted and the rest being sentenced to a total of 2,665 years in jail. Newspapers celebrated the victory, but the Italian people were less convinced in the finality of the trial. After the first maxi trial, two additional maxi trials were spun off and then prosecuted, soon leading to a fourth maxi trial in 1988. If this was a positive, a distinctive negative was that the Italian legal system allowed convicts out of jail during the appeals process, which meant that by 1989, only 60 of the 342 men originally convicted were actually still in prison.

While all this was taking place, Falcone's power within the judicial system was weakening. He was passed up for an important position, a decision that did not just hurt him professionally. More than a matter of pride, Falcone believed that being slighted for an important government role meant that the mafia would see him as not being supported by the state and, thus, vulnerable. With eerie foresight he told a friend of his, "I am a dead man." Soon, his fears were confirmed when he found a gym bag packed with explosives near his beach house.

In 1991, the tides of anti-mafia activity turned when Italian politics started to shift after the end of the cold war. Finally back in the government's good graces, Falcone was invited to become the Director of Penal Affairs, with the hopes that he could stem a new wave of violence that threatened to weaken public support for the government. Although his friends were worried about the possible implications for his safety, Falcone accepted the post. Within a year, he started to set up two major government organizations that are still the cornerstone of the Italian anti-mafia machine: the DIA (the Italian equivalent to the FBI) and the DNA, an anti-mafia prosecutors office that was enlisted to create a computer database on organized crime. While all this was going on, Falcone and Borsellino finally won a definitive verdict on their original case, which meant that many of their defendants would now be serving life sentences. It had taken 130 years, but the Italian state had finally managed to acknowledge that the Sicilian mafia was a true, organized entity that posed a dire threat to the health of the nation. However, no sooner did the court hand out its verdict than the death sentences against Falcone and Borsellino were reactivated. Falcone was murdered, Borsellino was selected to replace him, and by the next summer, he too was dead.[207]

After the murders of Falcone and Borsellino, Italy was forced to take notice. Since the mafia was an organization of silence communicating through its actions, experts puzzled over the true meaning of these spectacular killings. Much was made of the fact that they had chosen to kill Falcone in Palermo when it would have been simpler to attack him in Rome, where he lived and traveled without bodyguards. The conclusion that one mafia informant - once again, the infamous Tommaso Buscetta - came to was that the mafia resorted to these large-scale, public killings rather than maintain their low profile because it was struggling to survive. Though at the time he was laughed at, in the end his evaluation proved to be spot-on. The mafia was in crisis because its relationship with the Christian Democratic Party had begun to fray, and it needed to strike at the highest levels of the state because it was no longer able to protect it.

The Italian state snapped to action in the wake of the killings, if only to send a clear message to the Italian people that they were not complicit in these horrific deaths. The city of Palermo rose

---

[207] Dickie, *Blood Brothers,* 297-310.

up in protest, and people used the names Falcone and Borsellino as a rallying cry for their own commitment to fight the Cosa Nostra. For their part, Parliament quickly passed the aggressive anti-mafia measures it had long stalled on, including laws that changed prison conditions in order to make sure that mafiosi would be unable to continue running their empire from behind bars, as they had in the past. It also committed to sending 7,000 armed troops to Sicily to establish roadblocks and provide protection, freeing up the police to work on investigations. The DIA and the DNA, the anti-mafia institutions that Falcone himself had created, were called in to work to find the killers and to try to bring them to justice.

Over the course of the next two years, hundreds of mafiosi turned against the organization as cooperating witnesses, either because they themselves feared the tough new conditions of the Italian state or because they were increasingly unsettled by the tough, unrelenting tactics of the bosses. Thanks to their help, the police were able to dismantle whole organizations and managed to track down over 300 fugitives.

At the same time, the Italian government went through its own period of much needed cleansing, known as Operation Clean Hands (in Italian, *mani pulite*), in which a third of the national Parliament and half of the Sicilian Parliament was being criminally investigated.[208] The longtime leader of the Christian Democrat Party and former prime minister, Giulio Andreotti,[209] was accused of collusion with the mafia, leading quickly to the dissolution of Italy's most powerful post-war political party.[210] Ironically, just as the Italian state was actually trying to do something about the mafia, it was itself being dissolved, a clear case of too little, too late.

In 1993, the Italian government got a major victory when it captured the boss of all bosses, Toto Riina, thanks to a betrayal from a mafioso on the run from his vengeance. He was captured while stopped at a traffic light and offered no resistance to his arrest, after almost three decades on the run from the law. He died in prison in 2017, but his family members that inherited control of the organization decided to carry on with his violent tactics, considering such efforts including bombing the Leaning Tower of Pisa, poisoning children's snacks, and endeavoring to spread HIV through dirty syringes on beaches. In the end, they decided to bomb the car of a TV personality, Maurizio Costanzo, who had made anti-mafia remarks (he was unhurt), and they set off several other bombs, including in Florence (five killed, forty wounded) and in the Roman soccer stadium (it failed to go off). In this period, thanks to its relentless violence, the Cosa Nostra suffered another setback: the rebuke of the church that had previously been reticent to speak out on such volatile, secular matters.

Now that the verdicts of the maxi trials had definitively confirmed the existence of the Cosa Nostra, they no longer had to hide in the shadows. This meant that they were able to be more

---

[208] Stille 1996:6
[209] For the most readable account of Andreotti and his relationship to Sicily, see Robb, 2014.
[210] Stille 1996:421

overtly violent, but it also meant that they were undermining the institutional ties they had long cultivated. No longer could they rely on support from (or silence on the part of) many institutions and even the church. *Pentiti* started coming forward left and right, all the way up to some of the most senior men of honor.

In 1995, shockingly enough, Italy's longtime prime minister, Giulio Andreotti, was put on trial for his involvement with the mafia, in what was called the trial of the century. He was charged with associating with some of the worst mafiosi of Italian history, including a secret encounter during which he supposedly kissed Totò Riina in an act of deference. Prosecutors accused Andreotti of being beloved in the Cosa Nostra, whose members referred to him as "Uncle Giulio." In 1999, after four years, Andreotti was found innocent, as the mafia witnesses were deemed unreliable. Nonetheless, this verdict did not truly exonerate him, as his defense was simply the fact that he found Sicilian affairs too complicated to deal with and that he delegated that work to his lieutenant (who had conveniently been murdered). The not-guilty verdict was confirmed in May 2003, and tThe celebrated 2008 film, *Il divo*, directed by Paolo Sorrentino is another fascinating look at (and condemnation of) the connection between Andreotti and the mafia. All that the judges could say was that Andreotti would have to "answer to history."[211]

---

[211] Dickie 2015: 320-324.

Andreotti

Without a doubt, 1992-1994 represented a major downturn for the Cosa Nostra, which is still functioning today. Anti-mafia efforts resulted in 1,200 collaborators coming forward to testify against the Cosa Nostra just a few years later in 1997.[212] During the rise of Prime Minister Silvio Berlusconi, a number of important legal decisions codified anti-mafia decrees into permanent laws, suggesting that the grip was tightening around them. New laws have since been enacted to try to keep imprisoned bosses from running their empires from behind bars, as their predecessors had done. These efforts continue in the United States and Italy, with major arrests and imprisonment happening recently in Catania and Palermo. On May 30, 2019, 11 suspected mafioso were arrested for suspicion of illegal activities regarding the management of one of Sicily's largest natural parks. This was obviously a positive development, but it was also a sign that the mafia is still up and running.[213]

Another recent Cosa Nostra scam involves diverting funds for clean energy development such as wind turbines, in which communities with little wind power receive large grants to harness it.[214] In a fitting irony, on July 17, 2019, the day that Andrea Camilleri, one of Sicily's most beloved anti-mafia authors, died at age of 93, 15 more suspected mafiosi, based in Palermo, were arrested in coordinated raids by Italian police officers and FBI agents in both countries. In Palermo, this included Thomas Gambino, considered to be one of the most important members of the notorious Gambino crime family.[215]

Even as they show their capacity for adapting themselves to whatever new industry they might need to engage, the Cosa Nostra also faces increasing competition from other Italian and global mafias, such as the Calabrian 'ndrangheta, now the most powerful criminal organization in Italy. Thus, despite its long history, it is unlikely the Sicilian organization will ever return to its former glory, but the Cosa Nostra continues to make life on the island of Sicily worse for the people who live there. Its members still demand the *pizzo,* hinder much needed construction projects, destroy natural landmarks for gain or for vendetta, and depress the tourism economy as archeological and architectural treasures are allowed to degrade into slums.[216] Even if they are no longer what they once were, their power is such that one ex-mafioso declared, "In my area, you can't move a pin without Cosa Nostra."[217]

Over the course of its more than a century and a half-long existence, the Sicilian Cosa Nostra has taken on many different industries - from lemons to narcotics to concrete - and spread across

---

[212] Schneider and Schneider 2003:132

[213] Paris, 2019.

[214] https://www.lavoce.info/archives/60305/vento-sporco-le-mani-della-mafia-nelleolico/

[215] https://www.cbsnews.com/news/mafia-raids-italy-us-arrest-thomas-gambino-inzerillo-organized-crime-family-cosa-nostra-palermo-sicily-2019-7-17/

[216] Stille 1996:12

[217] Stille 1996:11

the Atlantic. It has murdered judges and politicians, their own members, law enforcement, and even children, but it has never changed its fundamental principles or objectives: to amass power, murdering all those who get in their way.[218]

Thanks to this long, bloody history, the Cosa Nostra remains the most famous of all the mafias worldwide. However, in practical terms, they simply cannot compete with the massive global juggernaut that the Neapolitan Camorra and the Calabrian 'ndrangheta have become. Along with the mafia's legacy of thousands of deaths and the gutting of Palermo's urban fabric, the Cosa Nostra has irrevocably damaged the reputation of the Sicilian people - the primary victims of their activity - to the extent that being considered a mafioso is a regional trait.

Through it all, the Cosa Nostra continues to benefit from dramatic representations in the media, from Mario Puzo's *The Godfather* and the subsequent film trilogy to *The Sopranos* television series. These stories have tended to glorify the violence and make engaging in this behavior seem commonplace for the Sicilians and the Sicilian Americans.[219] Scholars have studied this, working to demystify the mafioso by analyzing the way these stereotypes have been constructed and spread.[220]

While it is important to point a finger at commercial representations for their role in glorifying the violent Cosa Nostra brand, it is also important to consider the way the Sicilian Mafia spread as the result of complex, interweaving of political circumstances. Northern Italy often looks at the mafia as a symptom of Southern corruption, but the Piedmont-based government was very much responsible for setting the stage for the mafia's early development. Such decisions as focusing on infrastructure improvements in the north while the south faced droughts no doubt did much to help advance the mafia's cause, as did the imposition of martial law, making the state appear more unlawful than the supposed bandits they were persecuting. [221] Furthermore, it is important not to forget the roles of the Allied army and the American government in supporting the Cosa Nostra, as detailed by one British Allied intelligence officer, Norman Lewis, who went on to write a history of the Sicilian Mafia and a novel inspired by it.[222] After the war, the mafia continued to ensure its survival thanks to its relationship with powerful politicians, namely with the Christian Democrats, who were bolstered – in turn – by the American government, based on its belief they would collectively be a bulwark against communism.

Approaching his death in 2000, the famous mafioso informant Tommaso Buscetta declared that the Cosa Nostra had won because "the mafia is inborn in all Sicilians."[223] As much as the mafia's success clearly depended on circumstance and strategic affiliation with institutional powers, the

---

[218] Dickie 2015:26
[219] Dainotto 2015:preface
[220] Coluccello 2016. See also Dainotto, 2015.
[221] De Stefano 2007:21
[222] See Lewis, 1964. See also Lewis, 1986.
[223] Dickie 2015: 337.

fact of its continued survival to the present day means that people must continue to search for answers within the Cosa Nostra itself,[224] in the hope that one day, someone will figure out how to dismantle it once and for all.[225]

The Camorra Today

Today the Camorra bears little resemblance to the original society that was born in filth of the Bourbon prisons. After a series of blows and its apparent demise in the post-unification and fascist era, the Camorra refashioned itself. This does not appear to have been a concerted, strategic effort, but rather a matter of happenstance. The small-time criminals who were able to adopt a new identity managed to bring the Camorra back to life, growing it into a stronger, more insidious organization. Gone are the rituals and dagger duels, ranks, and codes. Instead, the Camorra now refers to a largely unstable network of gangster syndicates that constantly changes territorial holdings over the Campania region. Many of their illegal activities are the same, but they are much more successful and powerful than their predecessors were, even if individual clans might have a significantly shorter time in power.

After a major clan war in the late 1980s and the crackdown on the Sicilian Cosa Nostra in the wake of some high-profile assassinations, the explicit use of violence by mafias in Italy has decreased in general, most notably the number of homicides. With that said, even if the overall number of violent crimes decreased amongst all the mafias in Italy, the Camorra is believed to have been responsible for approximately half of the mafia murders committed in that time,[226] and while a crackdown was happening in Italy, the Camorra was busy establishing itself all across Europe. France, the United Kingdom, Austria, Portugal, Holland, and Scotland were all known to be countries in which the Camorra was able to traffic drugs and launder money through pizzerias, restaurants and stores, marking the first steps in their attempts to penetrate foreign economies at other levels. Switzerland served as a base for their massive laundering operations, Western Europe was the main focus of their drug-trafficking routes, and Eastern Europe (especially the Czech Republic) was where they focused on prostitution and the sale of counterfeit goods.[227]

Given that all this has been available since the mid-1990s, it is at least somewhat surprising that decades later, authorities are still unable to fully understand the true extent of the reach of the Camorra in Europe and beyond. Mafia scholars and law enforcement bodies still disagree over whether the Camorra's main seat of power remains in southern Italy or whether the organization is truly as global as it attempts to suggest.[228] Regardless, this uncertainty is itself a

---

[224] One recent, highly technical attempt to define the Sicilian Mafia can be found in Scalia, 2016.
[225] On current anti-mafia efforts, see

[226] Massari and Martone, "Doing Research on Mafia Violence: An Introduction," 3.
[227] Felia Allum, *The Invisible Camorra: Neapolitan Crime Families across Europe* (Ithaca, NY: Cornell University Press, 2016), 2.

benefit for the Camorra. Control of a territory was a major part of the early Camorra activity, but today deterritorialization has become a central strategy, together with a desire for invisibility, rather than the ostentatious bling of past bosses. After all, it is much more difficult for governments to fight what they cannot see.[229]

An apt example to contrast the Camorra of today with the Camorra of the post-war period comes in the figure of Paolo Di Lauro,[230] the leader of the powerful clan that operates in the northern suburbs of Naples. Unlike Raffaele Cutolo, who bought himself a castle, Di Lauro is a low profile figure, so much so that he was unheard of until a feud exploded in his territory in the early 2000s and resulted in 100 dead bodies. Hailing from humble origins, Di Lauro began his career as a smuggler but quickly rose through the ranks when he killed his boss and oriented the clan towards drug importing and dealing. He avoided getting involved in protection rackets and territorial skirmishes, steering clear of other powerful clans until he was able to buy their support with his massive profits. Di Lauro is known for introducing the network-based business model, whereby drug zones were "rented" to outside operators who paid the clan a monthly fee. Di Lauro worked to cultivate a "brand" that worked through what was effectively franchising, and this kind of compartmentalization allowed it to avoid a major legal takedown.[231]

Throughout the history of the mafia, the most detailed accounts of the activity of the Camorra come through repentant members who, for that reason alone, could not be fully trusted. However, in the early 2000s, a man named Roberto Saviano made a major splash when he published the book *Gomorra*,[232] which was based on his years at the fringes of the Camorra. He embedded himself into the Camorra as a journalist and subsequently earned himself a spot on the Camorra's hitlist, which has necessitated his living with a police escort ever since its publication. In the book, which was widely translated and adapted into an acclaimed 2008 film by director Matteo Garrone,[233] Saviano detailed the modern development of the Camorra, which he claims the organization's members call "il Sistema" ("the system"). If he's correct, it's an apt term to describe this diffuse network with no clear leader or unified structure.

Among the various episodes, Saviano wrote about the monopolization of the waste management industry, which took poisonous byproducts from the north and illegally disposed of them in the south, contaminating the food that Italians then eat. He also highlighted some of the more recent enterprises of the Camorra, including its involvement in the garment industry,

---

228 Allum, *The Invisible Camorra*, 3.

229 Brancaccio, "Violent Contexts and Camorra Clans," 139.

230 Simone Di Meo, *L'impero della camorra: vita violenta del boss Paolo Di Lauro* (Newton Compton, 2008).

231 Brancaccio, "Violent Contexts and Camorra Clans," 140.

232 Roberto Saviano, *Gomorrah: A Personal Journey into the Violent International Empire of Naples' Organized Crime System* (New York: Farrar, Straus and Giroux, 2007). Saviano's next book covered the illegal cocaine trade and its relationship to Naples: Roberto Saviano, *ZeroZeroZero: Look at Cocaine and All You See Is Powder. Look Through Cocaine and You See the World* (New York: Penguin, 2016).

233 Simona Bondavalli, "Waste Management: Garbage Displacement and the Ethics of Mafia Representation in Matteo Garrone's Gomorra," *California Italian Studies* 2, no. 1 (2011), https://escholarship.org/uc/item/9dz1s5kc.

operated by means of labor provided by profoundly exploited Chinese immigrants. Some of the most disturbing pages of his book include anecdotes about gangsters who are barely older than children and who play with machine guns as if they were toys as they quote lines from famous mafia movies. It's a stark reminder that demonstrates how the cinematic glorification of criminal organizations is not just harmless entertainment, but has, in fact, influenced a new generation of mobsters, many of whom will never get the chance to grow up into adults.

Together with specific, horrific accounts of violence, Saviano's harsh account is devastating in that it shows the system's involvement at every level of society. It is no longer just a problem in the city of Naples or the surrounding countryside; indeed, it makes the days of the mozzarella racket look quaint. Instead, "the system" is deeply implicated in the entire economy of Italy internally, and also in terms of its relationship to the global economy. Saviano laid out how the system negatively influences the food the Italian people eat, the clothes they wear, and even where they put their trash. Like it or not, no one is exempt from the Camorra's reach.

Given that he is a character in his own book, Saviano has come under scrutiny in recent years, and some people have challenged the specific details of his book, including the fact that it was published as non-fiction. Today, it is generally accepted as fictionalized reporting, but even if the absolute specifics of Saviano's gruesome, depressing account of the Camorra cannot be taken as fully accurate, his portrayal of the contemporary underworld is fundamentally accurate.[234]

Even if it remains rooted in Naples, the Camorra has its tentacles in projects across the globe, and as the Camorra bosses spread their criminal organization abroad, they keep a careful watch on potentially lucrative dealings that are going on in their own backyard, which means that the surrounding areas of Naples are not exempt from the meddling of the Camorra. In 2013, an investigation was opened into the mysteriously ballooning costs surrounding the World Heritage Organization site at Pompeii, where mafia involvement was suspected.[235]

Meanwhile, in the years since, the Italian police have continued to round up Camorra members, charging them for a range of crimes such as extortion, drug trafficking, prostitution, and illegal waste disposal.[236] Nonetheless, unlike the Sicilian mafia whose "glory days" seem to be behind it, the Neapolitan Camorra appears to live on like a many-headed hydra, and thanks to its decentralized structure, no particular arrest can spell doom for the group. Instead, cutting off one head just seems to generate more.

---

[234] Luca Pocci, "'Io so': A Reading of Roberto Saviano's Gomorra," *Modern Language Notes* 126, no. 1 (2011): 224–44.

[235] Michael Day, "The Mafia Left Naples in Ruins. Can They Do the Same to Pompeii?," *The Independent; London (UK)*, April 22, 2013, sec. World.

[236] "Naples Mafia Suspects Arrested," *Irish Times; Dublin*, January 23, 2014. "Six Naples Mafia Suspects Arrested," *TCA Regional News; Chicago*, March 2, 2017, http://search.proquest.com/docview/1873360445/citation/3F90B52EDDB84D67PQ/1.

Through it all, the Neapolitan mafia continues to affect every level of society in Southern Italy. Its members have corrupted Italian institutions and repressed the ambitions of ordinary citizens. They have compromised the judicial system, wasted resources, and defiled precious landscapes. They have infiltrated the police, the various levels of government, and multiple sectors of the economy, and they have done all this in conjunction with the development of the modern state of Italy, the only modern Western European nation to suffer such a rash of criminal syndicates.[237] Described by one historian as an "underground river, emerging in different forms depending on particular historical phases and territories,"[238] the Camorra is perfectly positioned to exploit the global economy of today. Although the individual groups within it tend to have a short lifetime, they are able to be replaced frequently and regenerate themselves in the face of any adversity.[239] One can only guess how the Camorra will transform itself in the future.

The 'Ndrangheta in the 21st Century

Throughout most of its history, the 'Ndrangheta has been largely underestimated and elusive, despite the fact that in its earliest years it faced the kind of major prosecutions that the other mafias were able to evade through corruption and intimidation. However, in the 21st century, the group's profile changed dramatically after the murder of Francesco Fortugno, the President of the Regional Council of Calabria, and the Duisburg massacre.

On October 16, 2005, in the town of Locri, Fortugno was killed in front of his polling place while he was surrounded by other people. It was a deliberately public killing, and the mafiosi chose to conduct it in that manner despite the fact that they were plenty familiar with easier ways to murder a victim. Put simply, the Fortugno murder was committed in order to send a message to Calabrian politicians about who was truly in charge.[240]

Less than two years later, on August 15, 2007, six Italian men were killed in a small German town named Duisburg after celebrating one of their birthdays at a restaurant. The two assailants fired upwards of 70 shots at the victims, one of whom was just 18. When the police found the bodies, they saw a partly burned image of Archangel Michael, signifying that the 18-year-old had been initiated into the Honored Society that day.[241]

This was the worst mafia killing outside of Italy and the United States, and it was clear that the 'Ndrangheta was responsible for it. For the first time, Europe was forced to take notice of the organization that had long been in the shadows, but was now the richest and most powerful mafia in Italy.[242] In the 1980s, a prosecutor in Florida had quipped, "The 'Ndrangheta is as

---

[237] Dickie, *Blood Brotherhoods,* xxvii.
[238] Brancaccio, "Violent Contexts and Camorra Clans," 136.
[239] Brancaccio, "Violent Contexts and Camorra Clans," 141.
[240] Ciconte, 45-6.
[241] Dickie, *Blood Brotherhoods,* xxxix.
[242] Dickie, *Blood Brotherhoods,* xxxiv.

invisible as the other side of the moon."[243] After the massacre, this no longer held true.

Soon, law enforcement agencies began to focus on the 'Ndrangheta, not just in Italy but also in the United States. Just one year after the massacre, a Wikileaks disclosure publicized that the United States Consul General had this to say about Calabria and its powerful mafia: "The 'ndrangheta organized crime syndicate controls vast portions of [Calabria's] territory and economy, and accounts for at least three% of Italy's GDP (probably much more) through drug trafficking, extortion and usury…Much of the region's industry collapsed over a decade ago, leaving environmental and economic ruin. The region comes in last place in nearly every category of national economic assessments. Most of the politicians we met on a recent visit were fatalistic, of the opinion that there was little that could be done to stop the region's downward economic spiral or the stranglehold of the 'ndrangheta. A few others disingenuously suggested that organized crime is no longer a problem… No one believes the central government has much, if any, control of Calabria, and local politicians are uniformly seen as ineffective and/or corrupt. If Calabria were not part of Italy, it would be a failed state."[244]

In the wake of the Fortugno killing and the Duisburg massacre, law enforcement agencies, investigators, and those who study the 'Ndrangheta have been left with unanswered questions about the future of the organization. The two events signaled a major change in the 'Ndrangheta, particularly in terms of the spectacular killings in a foreign country, which represented a blatant disregard of their traditional desire for secrecy. Some speculated that it was a sign that parts of the 'Ndrangheta were preparing to leave Calabria and use foreign countries as bases for new operations. However, in the aftermath, it appears that a peace deal was brokered within the 'Ndrangheta in order to assure newfound stability. This appears to have been a successful strategy, especially in the wake of the global financial crisis that began in 2007 and 2008. 'Ndrangheta was able to take advantage of its deep involvement in diverse financial sectors, propelling itself to even greater heights.[245]

In the case of the Sicilian mafia, mob insiders thought the spectacular killings of the 1990s were a sign of growing desperation. However, Barreca disagreed with this perspective when he discussed the 'Ndrangheta; instead, he believed that the high-profile killings are an effort to establish a dialogue with the government and essentially force them into a conversation. According to Barreca, it is the dialogue itself that is important, more than what is actually talked about, because it is a sign of the 'Ndrangheta's legitimacy. If the government is compelled to negotiate with the organization, it will be acknowledging the fact that the mafiosi have managed to integrate themselves into society.[246]

As the Calabrian mafia has grown, there are signs of change in their impoverished region, but

[243] Varese, *Mafias on the Move, How Organized Crime Conquers New Territories*, 32.
[244] John Dickie, *Blood Brotherhoods: A History of Italy's Three Mafias* (PublicAffairs, 2014), xxvii.
[245] Ciconte, 45-49.
[246] Antonelli and Nuzzi, *Blood Ties*.

not the kinds that promise real improvement. Cheaply made houses are still crumbling, but some of them have cars worth 200,000 euros pulling into their garages. Streets are laden with potholes, but some homes have golden faucets.[247]

Today, more than a decade after the Duisburg massacre shocked the world, the 'Ndrangheta shows no signs of slowing despite constant efforts and occasional victories on the part of law enforcement. For example, on July 18, 2019, 14 suspected members of the Calabrian Honored Society were arrested in Canada. Considered the founding members of the Canadian branch of the 'Ndrangheta, they face charges including association with a transnational, armed mafia, illegal arms trafficking, fraudulent money transfers, manipulation of credit, and usury.[248] A recent study suggested that in 2013, thanks to a healthy business model that includes extortion, usury, gambling, prostitution, and the trafficking of drugs and people, the 'Ndrangheta managed to earn more than $75.3 billion, equaling the revenues of McDonald's and Deutsche Bank combined. That figure would also equate to 3.5% of Italy's GDP that year. These figures are still a subject of debate, especially since there is obviously no official records for the profits of the criminal organization, but even if they are an overestimation, they give a sense of the magnitude of the problem.[249]

Although the Italian mafias are products of the 19th century and all the political and social upheaval that took place in the south of Italy, they have distinctly different histories at any given point in time. To determine why, historians have combed the little documentary evidence available and have turned to the few *pentiti* who are still alive and willing to collaborate.[250] What they have been able to conclude when it comes to the 'Ndrangheta is that the most powerful mafia in Italy acquired its status thanks to its extreme reliability. That reliability is the byproduct of several factors, including: a tight family structure; the commitment to *omertà*; its strategic positioning when the Cosa Nostra was being prosecuted in the 1990s for the Borsellino and Falcone assassinations; its flexible but sturdy hierarchy; and its ability to export and replicate itself within Italy and abroad.

Thus, even as the 'Ndrangheta never attracted the same level of interest as the other Italian mafias - there are no famous Hollywood films or Italian novels about the group like there are for the Cosa Nostra and the Camorra – the organization's low profile, carefully and cultivated for several decades, may have made the organization unstoppable in the 21st century.[251] Today, it is believed that there are approximately 86 different mafia families operating in the province of Reggio Calabria alone, to say nothing of the way the organization has metastasized across the world.[252] Only time will tell if that global reach will shrink or grow, but nothing in the

---

[247] Antonelli and Nuzzi.

[248] https://www.repubblica.it/cronaca/2019/07/18/news/ndrangheta_canadian_connection_-231457811/

[249] https://www.vice.com/en_us/article/9bz3ny/ndrangheta-mafia-italy-calabria-mcdonalds-drugs

[250] Dickie, *Blood Brotherhoods*, xxvii.

[251] Sergi and Lavorgna, *'Ndrangheta*, 2.

[252] Varese, *Mafias on the Move, How Organized Crime Conquers New Territories*, 33.

'Ndrangheta's history suggests it is going away anytime soon.

Online Resources

<u>Other books about organized crime</u> by Charles River Editors

<u>Other books about the Camorra on Amazon</u>

<u>Other books about Cosa Nostra on Amazon</u>

<u>Other books about the 'Ndrangheta on Amazon</u>

Further Reading about Cosa Nostra

Bolzoni, Attilio, and Giuseppe D'Avanzo. *The Boss of Bosses: The Life of the Infamous Toto Riina Dreaded Head of the Sicilian Mafia*. Orion Publishing Group, 2015.

Cawthorne, Nigel. *Mafia: The History of the Mob*. London: Arcturus Publishing, 2012.

Coluccello, Rino. *Challenging the mafia Mystique: Cosa Nostra from Legitimisation to Denunciation*. Springer, 2016.

Dainotto, Roberto M. *The mafia: A Cultural History*. Reaktion Books, 2015.

Davis, John A. *Naples and Napoleon: Southern Italy and the European Revolutions, 1780-1860*. Oxford, UK: Oxford University Press, 2006.

Davis-Secord, Sarah. *Where Three Worlds Met: Sicily in the Early Medieval Mediterranean*. Cornell, NY: Cornell University Press, 2017.

De Stefano, George. *An Offer We Can't Refuse: The mafia in the Mind of America*. New York: Faber & Faber/Farrar, Straus, Giroux, 2007.

Dickie, J. *Darkest Italy: The Nation and Stereotypes of the Mezzogiorno, 1860-1900*. Springer, 1999.

Dickie, John. *Cosa Nostra: A History of the Sicilian Mafia*. New York: St. Martin's Press, 2015.

Fentress, James. *Rebels and mafiosi: Death in a Sicilian Landscape*. Ithaca, NY: Cornell University Press, 2018.

Follain, Jochn. *Vendetta: The mafia, Judge Falcone and the Quest for Justice*. Hodder & Stoughton, 2012.

Heartfield, James. *An Unpatriotic History of the Second World War*. John Hunt Publishing, 2012.

Lewis, Norman. *The Honoured Society: The mafia Conspiracy Observed*. Collins, 1964.

- - - . *The Sicilian Specialist*. Perseus Books Group, 1986.

Lupo, Salvatore. *History of the mafia*. New York: Columbia University Press, 2011.

- - - . *Storia della mafia: dalle origini ai giorni nostri*. Rome: Donzelli Editore, 2004.

- - - . *The Two Mafias: A Transatlantic History, 1888-2008*. Springer, 2015.

Maselli, Joseph, and Dominic Candeloro. *Italians in New Orleans*. Arcadia Publishing, 2004.

Montanelli, Indro, and Mario Cervi. *L'Italia degli anni di piombo - 1965-1978*. Bur, 2013.

Newark, Tim. *The mafia at War: The Shocking True Story of America's Wartime Pact with Organized Crime*. Skyhorse Publishing Inc., 2012.

Niceforo, Alfredo. *L'Italia barbara contemporanea: (studi ed appunti)*. Remo Sandron, 1898.

Paris, Michele. "Le mani di Cosa Nostra sui fondi europei, undici arresti in Sicilia." *euronews*, May 30, 2019. https://it.euronews.com/2019/05/30/le-mani-di-cosa-nostra-sui-fondi-europei-undici-arresti-in-sicilia.

Pickering-Iazzi, Robin. *The Italian Antimafia, New Media, and the Culture of Legality*. University of Toronto Press, 2017.

- - - . *The mafia in Italian Lives and Literature: Life Sentences and Their Geographies*. University of Toronto Press, 2015.

Reppetto, Thomas. *American Mafia: A History of Its Rise to Power*. Henry Holt and Company, 2016.

Riall, Lucy. *Garibaldi: The Invention of a Hero*. New Haven: Yale University Press, 2008.

- - - . *Sicily and the Unification of Italy: Liberal Policy and Local Power, 1859-1866*. Oxford, UK: Oxford University Press Incorporated, 1998.

- - - . *The Italian Risorgimento: State, Society and National Unification*. New York: Routledge, 2002.

Robb, Peter. *Midnight In Sicily: On Art, Feed, History, Travel and La Cosa Nostra*. New York: Farrar, Straus and Giroux, 2014.

Scalia, Vincenzo. *Crime, Networks and Power: Transformation of Sicilian Cosa Nostra.* Springer, 2016.

Schneider, Jane, and Peter T. Schneider. *Reversible Destiny: Mafia, Antimafia, and the Struggle for Palermo.* Berkeley, CA: University of California Press, 2003.

Smith, Denis Mack. *Cavour and Garibaldi 1860: A Study in Political Conflict* (Cambridge, UK: Cambridge University Press, 1985).

Stille, Alexander. *Excellent Cadavers: The mafia and the Death of the First Italian Republic.* New York: Vintage Books, 1996.

Williams, Paul L. *Operation Gladio: The Unholy Alliance Between the Vatican, the CIA, and the mafia.* Prometheus Books, 2018.

Further Reading about 'Ndrangheta

Antonelli, Claudio, and Gianluigi Nuzzi. Blood Ties: The Calabrian Mafia. Pan Macmillan, 2012.

Ciconte, Enzo. "Origins and Development of the 'Ndrangheta." In The 'Ndrangheta and Sacra Corona Unita: The History, Organization and Operations of Two Unknown Mafia Groups, edited by Serenata, Nicoletta, 33–55. New York: Springer, 2014.

Dickie, John. Blood Brotherhoods: A History of Italy's Three Mafias. PublicAffairs, 2014.

Figliomeni, Vincent C. 'Ndrangheta of Calabria: Exploring a Pragmatic Approach to Confronting ... -. Bloomington, IN: Author House, 2019. https://books.google.com/books?id=aCugDwAAQBAJ&printsec=frontcover&dq=ndrangheta&hl=en&sa=X&ved=0ahUKEwjwmJL8677jAhXCWc0KHcuICugQ6AEIOzAD#v=onepage&q&f=false.

Paoli, Letizia. Mafia Brotherhoods: Organized Crime, Italian Style. Oxford University Press, 2008.

Parini, Ercole Giap. "'Ndrangheta. Multilevel Criminal System of Power and Economic Accumulation." In The 'Ndrangheta and Sacra Corona Unita: The History, Organization and Operations of Two Unknown Mafia Groups, edited by Nicoletta Serenata, 51–62. Studies of Organized Crime. Cham: Springer International Publishing, 2014. https://doi.org/10.1007/978-3-319-04930-4_4.

Possumato, Dan. King of the Mountains: The Remarkable Story of Giuseppe Musolino, Italy's Most Famous Outlaw. Smoky City Press, 2013.

Reski, Petra. The Honored Society: A Portrait of Italy's Most Powerful Mafia. PublicAffairs, 2013.

Rinaldi, Luca. "How the 'Ndrangheta Quietly Became the McDonald's of Mafias." Vice (blog), April 17, 2014. https://www.vice.com/en_uk/article/9bz3ny/ndrangheta-mafia-italy-calabria-mcdonalds-drugs.

Serenata, Nicoletta. "Introduction." In The 'Ndrangheta and Sacra Corona Unita: The History, Organization and Operations of Two Unknown Mafia Groups, edited by Serenata, Nicoletta, 1–13. New York: Springer, 2014.

Sergi, Anna. "The Evolution of the Australian 'Ndrangheta. An Historical Perspective." Australian and New Zealand Journal of Criminology 2015 48 (2014): 155–74.

———. "What's in a Name? Shifting Identities of Traditional Organized Crime in Canada in the Transnational Fight against the Calabrian 'Ndrangheta." Canadian Journal of Criminology and Criminal Justice 60, no. 4 (November 10, 2018): 427–54.

Sergi, Anna, and Anita Lavorgna. 'Ndrangheta: The Glocal Dimensions of the Most Powerful Italian Mafia. New York: Springer, 2016.

Siebert, Renate. "Mafia Women: The Affirmation of a Female Pseudo-Subject. The Case of the 'Ndrangheta." In Women and the Mafia, edited by Giovanni Fiandaca, 19–45. STUDIES IN ORGANIZED CRIME. New York, NY: Springer New York, 2007. https://doi.org/10.1007/978-0-387-36542-8_3.

Testa, Alberto, and Anna Sergi. Corruption, Mafia Power and Italian Soccer. Routledge, 2018.

Varese, Federico. Mafias on the Move, How Organized Crime Conquers New Territories. Course Book. Princeton: Princeton University Press, 2011. https://doi.org/10.1515/9781400836727.

Further Reading about the Camorra

Allum, Felia. Camorristi, Politicians and Businessmen: The Transformation of Organized Crime in Post-War Naples. New York: Routledge, 2017.

———. The Invisible Camorra: Neapolitan Crime Families across Europe. Ithaca, NY: Cornell University Press, 2016.

Barbagallo, Francesco. Storia della camorra. Gius.Laterza & Figli Spa, 2014.

Behan, Tom. See Naples and Die: The Camorra and Organized Crime. London ; New York: Tauris Parke Paperbacks, 2002.

———. *The Camorra: Political Criminality in Italy*. New York: Routledge, 2005.

Bondavalli, Simona. "Waste Management: Garbage Displacement and the Ethics of Mafia Representation in Matteo Garrone's Gomorra." *California Italian Studies* 2, no. 1 (2011). https://escholarship.org/uc/item/9dz1s5kc.

Brancaccio, Luciano. "Violent Contexts and Camorra Clans." In *Mafia Violence: Political, Symbolic, and Economic Forms of Violence in Camorra Clans*, edited by Monica Massari and Vittorio Martone, 135–53. New York: Routledge, 2018.

Castellano, Carolina. "The Fascist Anti-Mafia Operation in Campania, 1926-1927 - ProQuest." *Modern Italy: Journal of the Association for the Study of Modern Italy* 22, no. 4 (November 2017): 403–17.

Castromediano, Sigismondo. *Carceri e galere politiche*. Tip. editrice Salentina, 1896.

Cervantes, Miguel De. *Rinconete and Cortadillo*. CreateSpace Independent Publishing Platform, 2016.

Day, Michael. "The Mafia Left Naples in Ruins. Can They Do the Same to Pompeii?" *The Independent; London (UK)*. April 22, 2013, sec. World.

Di Gennaro, Giacomo, and Antonio La Spina. "Introduction. The Costs of Illegality: A Research Programme." In *Mafia-Type Organisations and Extortion in Italy: The Camorra in Campania*, edited by Giacomo Di Gennaro and Antonio La Spina. New York: Routledge, 2018.

Dickie, John. *Blood Brotherhoods: A History of Italy's Three Mafias*. PublicAffairs, 2014.

———. *Mafia Republic: Italy's Criminal Curse. Cosa Nostra, 'Ndrangheta and Camorra from 1946 to the Present*. Hodder & Stoughton, 2013.

Lewis, Norman. *Naples '44: A World War II Diary of Occupied Italy*. Boston, MA: Da Capo Press, 2004.

Marrazzo, Giuseppe. *Il camorrista. Vita segreta di don Raffaele Cutolo*. Tullio Pironti, 2005.

Massari, Monica, and Vittorio Martone. "Doing Research on Mafia Violence: An Introduction." In *Mafia Violence: Political, Symbolic, and Economic Forms of Violence in Camorra Clans*, edited by Massari Massari Monica and Vittorio Martone, 1–16. New York: Routledge, 2018.

Meo, Simone Di. *L'impero della camorra: vita violenta del boss Paolo Di Lauro*. Newton Compton, 2008.

Monnier, Marc. *La camorra: notizie storiche*. G. Barbèra, 1863.

"Naples Mafia Suspects Arrested." *Irish Times; Dublin*. January 23, 2014.

Pocci, Luca. "'Io so': A Reading of Roberto Saviano's Gomorra." *Modern Language Notes* 126, no. 1 (2011): 224–44.

Romano, Liborio. *Memorie politiche di Liborio Romano pubblicate per cura di Giuseppe Romano suo fratello, con note e documenti*. Giuseppe Marghieri, 1873.

Santino, Umberto. *Mafia and Antimafia: A Brief History*. Bloomsbury Publishing, 2015.

Saviano, Roberto. *Gomorrah: A Personal Journey into the Violent International Empire of Naples' Organized Crime System*. New York: Farrar, Straus and Giroux, 2007.

———. *ZeroZeroZero: Look at Cocaine and All You See Is Powder. Look Through Cocaine and You See the World*. New York: Penguin, 2016.

Sciarrone, Rocco. *Mafie vecchie, mafie nuove: radicamento ed espansione*. Donzelli, 2009.

"Six Naples Mafia Suspects Arrested." *TCA Regional News; Chicago*. March 2, 2017. http://search.proquest.com/docview/1873360445/citation/3F90B52EDDB84D67PQ/1.

Solórzano, Alonso de Castillo. *La garduña de Sevilla, y anzuelo de las bolsas*. Imprenta de la Viuda de Jordan é Hijos, 1844.

Free Books by Charles River Editors

We have brand new titles available for free most days of the week. To see which of our titles are currently free, click on this link.

Discounted Books by Charles River Editors

We have titles at a discount price of just 99 cents everyday. To see which of our titles are currently 99 cents, click on this link.

Printed in Great Britain
by Amazon